Endorsements for
How to Save The World in Six (Not So Easy) Steps

"David Schizer's important book provides invaluable wisdom in making nonprofits more effective. Schizer is a gifted writer and incisive thinker. You will want to add this book to your reading list and library."

–Robert Abrams, former Attorney General of New York

"David Schizer's new book defines issues in the nonprofit sector with clarity, offers wise counsel to board members and staff alike, and balances the more intellectual content with heart-warming and entertaining anecdotes along the way. Reading this book is a journey worth taking for any professional or volunteer leader who is striving to advance the mission of their organization with excellence."

–Rachel Garbow Monroe, President & CEO, The Harry and Jeanette Weinberg Foundation

"This book is a major contribution. Successful nonprofit leadership isn't easy. You may know it when you see it, but David Schizer explains how to do it."

–Lee Goldman, Cournand and Richards Professor and Dean Emeritus, Columbia University Faculties of Health Sciences and Medicine

"Schizer's 'six Ps' are essential. They will add value for a plethora of non-profits—from universities and hospitals, to community organizations and religious institutions."

–Jonathan S. Lavine, Co-Managing Partner, Bain Capital; Chair, Columbia University Board of Trustees; and Chair Emeritus, City Year

D0986084

"Even the most capable nonprofit leader can fall prey to common pitfalls. *How to Save the World* is a 'tough love' guide to success in running mission-driven organizations. This book is full of practical advice, brought to life through illuminating interviews and lessons drawn from David Schizer's own experiences leading nonprofits in multiple sectors. New and experienced nonprofit managers alike will find this candid and accessible desk companion to be an invaluable resource."

–Gillian Lester, Dean and Lucy G. Moses
Professor of Law, Columbia Law School

"David Schizer has written an excellent guide to the leadership and management of nonprofit institutions. Trustees and employees will find *How to Save the World* a highly instructive, inspiring, comprehensive and reader-friendly companion.

The handbook draws from David's own rich set of experiences in academic and humanitarian work and those of selected CEOs. The lessons he conveys to the reader are clearly drawn. They apply to any and all organizations, whatever their missions, age, size, and ambition.

Capturing such diversity and complexity in breezy, inviting prose and infusing it with his own personal history and deeply held values are no mean feats.

Schizer, the former dean and now professor at Columbia Law School, is hereby granted an A.

And, I do not grade on the curve!"

–Reynold Levy, former CEO of the Robin Hood Foundation,
Lincoln Center, the International Rescue Committee, 92NY,
and the AT&T Foundation, as well as the author of *Yours*
for the Asking* and *They Told Me Not to Take That Job

"Drawing on his own expertise and insights from other nonprofit leaders, David Schizer teaches a master class in what makes nonprofits successful."

–Joe Lieberman, former United States Senator, Connecticut

"This essential book offers a powerful and practical guide for nonprofits to thrive in the 21st Century. David Schizer gets right to the heart of the complexities of the nonprofit world. His detailed and actionable book is a true gift for the sector. Highly recommended."

–Henry Timms, President of Lincoln Center and Co-Founder of #GivingTuesday

"At its core, *How to Save the World* is about the difficult choices nonprofit leaders make every day in their commitment to create thriving communities. Every leader, nonprofit and for-profit, should make the choice to read and learn the valuable lessons that David Schizer presents. *How to Save the World* is a must-read for nonprofit and corporate executives alike."

–Jennifer Sampson, President and CEO, United Way of Metropolitan Dallas

"Serving on a nonprofit board is deeply fulfilling, but also really challenging. David Schizer offers invaluable guidance. Every board member should take his lessons to heart."

–Lisa Landau Carnoy, Chair Emerita, Columbia University Board of Trustees and Independent Director of the United States Soccer Federation

"As the CEO of a mission-driven nonprofit, I know all too well how important this guidance is so we can save the world together. I keep the six Ps on my desk and refer to them often. Thank you, David, for this incredible guidance."

–Carol Baldwin Moody, President and CEO of Legal Momentum, The Women's Legal Defense and Education Fund

HOW TO SAVE THE WORLD IN SIX

(Not So Easy)

STEPS

HOW TO SAVE THE WORLD IN SIX

(Not So Easy)

STEPS

BRINGING OUT THE BEST IN NONPROFITS

DAVID M. SCHIZER

PostHill
PRESS

A POST HILL PRESS BOOK
ISBN: 979-8-88845-188-5
ISBN (eBook): 979-8-88845-189-2

How to Save the World in Six (Not So Easy) Steps
Bringing Out the Best in Nonprofits
© 2023 by David M. Schizer
All Rights Reserved

Cover design by Hampton Lamoureux

Although every effort has been made to ensure that the personal and professional advice present within this book is useful and appropriate, the author and publisher do not assume and hereby disclaim any liability to any person, business, or organization choosing to employ the guidance offered in this book.

No part of this book may be reproduced, stored in a retrieval system, or transmitted by any means without the written permission of the author and publisher.

Post Hill Press
New York • Nashville
posthillpress.com

Published in the United States of America
1 2 3 4 5 6 7 8 9 10

To Meredith—
For all the wise counsel and inspiration and,
of course, for everything else…

CONTENTS

CHAPTER 1

INTRODUCTION

Inspiration and Frustration

OLGA LIVES IN BELARUS, where her government pension is just four dollars per day. Battling cancer, she can barely move on her own. When I visited her, I saw that she has no central heat, even though Belarusian winters are bone-chillingly cold. Instead, Olga (not her real name) relies on a primitive fireplace—a hole in the wall covered with a grate. She burns firewood for one hour in the morning and one hour at night. When I asked if she has enough wood, her brown eyes sparkled as she said, "It's more than some people have."

This wood comes from JDC, the international humanitarian organization I used to lead. JDC also provides Olga with food, medicine, and other necessities, as well as home care. JDC's full name is the American Jewish Joint Distribution Committee, and it is sometimes also called "the Joint." For over a century, JDC has worked in Europe, Israel, and across the globe—indeed, everywhere but the United States—to combat Jewish poverty, provide humanitarian aid to other vulnerable populations, and strengthen Jewish communities.

Olga is one of tens of thousands of elderly clients that JDC serves in the former Soviet Union. To meet their basic needs, JDC was spending

1

more than one-third of its budget during my years as CEO (increasing from $110 million in 2018 to $145 million in 2020). Without this aid, these desperately poor seniors would die.

The admiration and compassion I felt for Olga was simple, but the work to care for her was not. My colleagues constantly looked for better ways to help her and our other elderly clients in the region. But this wasn't the only thing on JDC's plate. Other vulnerable populations also need care, but JDC doesn't have the resources to help everyone. No nonprofit does. Should we focus on children instead? Or people with disabilities? These choices are agonizing, but we have to make them.

I'd been there before. Ten years earlier, I was Dean of Columbia Law School during the financial crisis of 2008. Our endowment contracted sharply, our fundraising dried up, and our students were suddenly having trouble getting jobs, so we had to do more with less. This meant scaling back valuable programs and laying off dedicated colleagues so we could fund other priorities and balance our budget. Years later, I still remember how I felt. It was like being hit in the gut with a two-by-four.

At both Columbia and JDC, my colleagues faced these choices with courage and discipline, looking for the least painful ways to save money. But unfortunately, there was still pain. To make room for things we *had* to do, we could no longer do other things we *wanted* to do.

A few weeks after visiting Olga, I happened to be at a conference where another organization was asking donors to fund a new initiative. "This is a worthwhile program," one of their funders replied, "but why do you need new funding? The cost of launching this program is less than 2 percent of your budget. If you think it's important, why don't you just cut something else and use the savings to fund this new idea?"

The response was as candid as it was jarring. "You've served on our board so you know how dysfunctional our governance can be," replied the other nonprofit's board chair. "It's very difficult for us to cut programs and redirect funds."

Come on, really? Of course it's difficult, but that's no excuse. To advance the mission, every nonprofit needs to make hard choices and change with the times. Unfortunately, not all of them do.

For me, these two memories—JDC's lifesaving work with Olga and the other nonprofit's broken budgetary process—sum up why nonprofits can be both inspiring and frustrating.

BRINGING OUT THE BEST IN NONPROFITS

So what should we do? Bringing out the best in nonprofits is critical because we rely so heavily on them. Many of us are born in nonprofit hospitals, educated in nonprofit universities, and inspired at nonprofit religious institutions. Nonprofits also address burning issues such as climate change, income inequality, and racial justice, even when the government is stymied by political divisions.

At a more basic level, many of us have causes we love to support. Committing time and money to them is one of the most fulfilling things in our lives. Through nonprofits, we can honor our ideals, join a community of like-minded people, and pursue our dreams.

To touch our lives in all these ways, the United States has over 1.5 million nonprofits. Every year, they spend more than $2.5 trillion, which is more than the GDP of Canada. More than 200 million Americans donate to nonprofits, representing 70 percent of the population, while 25 percent volunteer their time. A number of other countries also have large nonprofit sectors, including Belgium, Canada, Israel, Japan, Mozambique, and New Zealand.

Sometimes our faith in nonprofits is amply justified. The finest ones advance compelling missions and launch bold experiments.

But unfortunately, there are horror stories as well. Even beloved nonprofits are sometimes wracked by corruption and misconduct. Do you remember the "Varsity Blues" scandal, where families bribed their way into prestigious colleges? Or the child abuse scandal at a storied college football team? Or the allegations of sexual misconduct and

3

cover-ups at humanitarian organizations? Sadly, many volumes could be filled with scandals that have come to light at nonprofits over the years.

But the focus here is on something more mundane and, I suspect, a lot more pervasive: mediocrity instead of misconduct. Too many nonprofits don't advance their mission effectively. They deliver subpar results, are stuck in their ways, or are wracked with infighting.

How can nonprofits avoid these traps? This book identifies the root causes of common problems at nonprofits and explains how to solve them.

The defining feature of nonprofits is their goal. Instead of making money, they advance a mission. This presents a fundamental challenge: their performance can be quite hard to measure. Unlike for-profit firms, they can't use profitability or share prices, so it's not easy to know whether nonprofits are pursuing their mission the right way. As a result, unwise and self-interested choices are harder to expose, conflicts are more difficult to resolve, and there is less pressure to change with the times.

At nonprofits, flawed choices are not just more difficult to root out, but also more troubling. When a for-profit firm wastes money, the share price suffers. But when this happens at a nonprofit, the *mission* suffers. This means that diseases aren't treated, knowledge isn't advanced, vulnerable populations aren't served, religious teachings aren't shared, culture and art aren't celebrated, and communal bonds aren't forged. These missed opportunities are especially heart-wrenching because money is already tight at most nonprofits. Instead of wasting these scarce dollars, they need to make the most of them!

Fortunately, these problems aren't inevitable. This brings us to the central lesson of this book. To deal with these challenges, nonprofits have to do two things really well. First, they need to figure out the best way to advance their mission, setting the right priorities, testing new ways to implement them, and holding themselves accountable. When they fall short, they need to make changes.

Second, coming up with the right strategy is only half the battle. It won't succeed—and might never even be attempted—unless enough people believe in it: professionals and volunteers need to go the extra mile in implementing it, while donors have to be willing to fund it.

In short, the key is to figure out what to do, while also getting everyone on board to do it. If you think this is a tall order, you are right. The truth is, each of these two jobs is exquisitely difficult on its own, and the two together are harder still.

This book explains how to accomplish these twin goals, so nonprofits can chart the right course and bring everyone along. After laying out the key strengths and weaknesses of nonprofits in the next two chapters, the rest of this book recommends six ways to leverage these strengths and shore up the weaknesses. We can "save the world in six (not so easy) steps" with what I call "the Six Ps":

- **Plan**: Run a rigorous planning process.
- **Persevere**: Line up internal support.
- **Prioritize**: Set priorities with "the three questions."
- **Pivot**: Experiment and innovate.
- **Publicize**: Share ideas and hold yourself accountable.
- **Partner**: Raise more money by involving donors in the work.

As challenging as these steps can be, the good news is that they are a labor of love. When we are passionate about a nonprofit's mission, we want to advance it as effectively as possible. If we can reach more people, or if we can do more for the ones we reach, don't we want to do that? Don't we *need* to do that?

But a labor of love is still labor, so it isn't always fun. In committing to a cause, we may be following our hearts, but in doing the work and making decisions, we need to use our heads. The point is not to hold hands and celebrate our own good intentions, but to get the job done. (A friend says that I sound like his "cranky uncle" when I make this case. He's made me see my own cranky uncle in a whole new light.)

The insights in this book apply to every mission-driven nonprofit—from houses of worship and hospitals to schools, advocacy organizations, museums, and humanitarian organizations. Although nonprofits pursue a dazzling array of missions—and vary also in the size of their budgets, the beneficiaries they serve, the funding sources they tap, and the geographical range they cover—they all face the same fundamental challenges: figuring out the best way to pursue their mission and lining up support to do it. The "Six Ps" can help them all advance their mission more successfully. Some of the lessons here also apply to country clubs, trade associations, credit unions, and other nonprofits that are not mission-driven—and, for that matter, for-profit firms and government agencies—but they aren't the focus of this book.

NONPROFIT LEADERS IN THIS BOOK

Many ideas in this book come from my own experience. I served as Dean of Columbia Law School for ten years (from 2004 to 2014) and as CEO of JDC for three years (from 2017 through 2019) before returning to the Columbia faculty.

In addition, this book also offers insights from other nonprofit leaders. I interviewed a distinguished group of twenty-six men and women, who have collectively led more than thirty nonprofits (see sidebar). I also incorporate ideas from Justice Ruth Bader Ginsburg (RBG), which come from our many conversations over the years. (I was her law clerk during her second year on the U.S. Supreme Court).

Some of the organizations led by this group are large, while others are small. Some have been around for more than one hundred years, while others are start-ups. Pursuing a broad range of missions, they include the American Museum of Natural History, the Archdiocese of Newark, Columbia University Vagelos College of Physicians and Surgeons, Earthjustice, Lincoln Center for the Performing Arts, the NAACP Legal Defense and Education Fund, United Way of Metropolitan Dallas, and the YMCA.

Nonprofit Leaders Interviewed for This Book*

Leader	Nonprofits
Amy Barasch	Her Justice
Charles Best	DonorsChoose
Rabbi Aviad Bodner	Stanton Street Shul; Congregation Ramath Orah
Kristen Clarke	Lawyers' Committee for Civil Rights Under Law
Asha Curran	GivingTuesday
Judith Browne Dianis	Advancement Project
Eric Fingerhut	Hillel International; Jewish Federations of North America
Ellen Futter	American Museum of Natural History; Barnard College
Father Richard Gabuzda	Institute for Priestly Formation
Ruth Bader Ginsburg	ACLU Women's Rights Project
Lee Goldman	Columbia University Vagelos College of Physicians and Surgeons
Eric Goldstein	UJA-Federation of NY
Sarah Hemminger	Thread
Peter Lehner	Natural Resources Defense Council (NRDC); Earthjustice
Leonard Leo	The Federalist Society

---

* This group is twice as diverse as the pool of CEOs in the sector as a whole: 22 percent are people of color (compared with only 8 percent in the sector overall), while 44 percent are women (compared with 21 percent among all large U.S. nonprofits).

Reynold Levy	92NY; AT&T Foundation; International Rescue Committee; Lincoln Center for the Performing Arts; Robin Hood Foundation
Rachel Garbow Monroe	Harry and Jeanette Weinberg Foundation
Wes Moore	BridgeEdU; Robin Hood Foundation; Governor of Maryland
Carol Baldwin Moody	Legal Momentum
Ruth Raskas	UJA-Federation of NY; Jewish Federations of North America
Jay Ruderman	Ruderman Family Foundation
Shira Ruderman	Ruderman Family Foundation
Bishop Michael Saporito	Archdiocese of Newark
Jennifer Sampson	United Way of Metropolitan Dallas
Theodore Shaw	NAACP Legal Defense and Education Fund
Henry Timms	92NY; Lincoln Center for the Performing Arts
Kevin Washington	YMCA

To sum up, keeping nonprofits on track is critically important, but also thoroughly difficult. This book recommends six ways to bring out the best in nonprofits. Before turning to these "Six Ps," let's start by looking at the core strengths and weaknesses of nonprofits. What strengths can we leverage? What weaknesses do we need to address?

CHAPTER 2

THE BEST OF TIMES

Strengths of Nonprofits

CHARLES LI STARTED HIS first job when he was sixteen years old, working on an oil rig in the North China Sea. During breaks, while others were smoking or playing cards, he taught himself English. Charles eventually became a journalist and met Randy Edwards, who ran Columbia Law School's Center for Chinese Legal Studies. Recognizing Charles's considerable talent, Randy arranged a scholarship for him.

Just eight years after graduating from law school, Charles became President of Merrill Lynch China. He went on to serve as Chairman of JP Morgan China and then as the longest-serving CEO in the history of the Hong Kong Stock Exchange. "Everything started for me fundamentally at Columbia Law School," Charles told an audience at the school in March of 2015. His loyalty to Columbia motivated him to serve on the University's board of trustees.

I know countless graduates like Charles whose scholarships helped them achieve remarkable success—as prominent lawyers, judges, business leaders, public servants, academics, and nonprofit leaders. A few thousand dollars of financial aid utterly changed their lives, empowering them to make their mark in the world. This is one of the things I love about universities.

Fortunately, this sort of inspiring story is common in nonprofits. But the truth is, not everything about nonprofits is inspiring. We want them to work miracles, but sometimes they just waste money. Even as some thrive on idealism and experimentation, others are mired in infighting and stagnation. Indeed, when another Charles—Charles Dickens—wrote that "It was the best of times, it was the worst of times," he could easily have been talking about nonprofits.

So how can we get the most out of nonprofits? We need to understand their strengths so we can take full advantage of them. At the same time, we also have to recognize their weaknesses so we can shore them up.

In fact, the strengths and weaknesses of nonprofits are often two sides of the same coin: the same qualities that inspire us also can be a source of frustration. Let's focus on five of these "mixed blessings":

- **Mission and Goals**: Nonprofits exist to pursue their missions. Some causes are inspiring, but others are stale or even misguided.
- **Motivation**: Nonprofit professionals and volunteers usually are motivated by idealism, not money. While this often drives them to deliver outstanding results, it sometimes makes them dogmatic and inflexible.
- **Diversity**: Nonprofits can be a powerful way to promote diversity. They have the autonomy to serve specific communities, and each community is free to form their own nonprofit. Yet unfortunately, this autonomy sometimes morphs into insularity.
- **Autonomy**: Nonprofits have the independence to advance novel causes and experiment with new approaches, but this autonomy also limits their accountability. This is especially problematic because progress at nonprofits can be difficult to measure, so misguided choices are harder to expose.

- **Funding:** Since funding is supplied voluntarily, funders often find profound satisfaction in providing this support. Yet raising this money is a challenge, which diverts scarce resources from the mission.

This chapter focuses on the bright side of these five defining features of nonprofits, while chapter 3 focuses on their dark side. After analyzing these singular strengths and weaknesses, this book explains how to tap a nonprofit's potential while steering clear of common pitfalls.

MISSION AND GOALS

Let's turn to the first singular strength of nonprofits. If you ask someone why they support a particular nonprofit—and, indeed, what they love about it—the answer is almost always the same: the cause.

There is something for everyone in the nonprofit sector's glittering mosaic of good work. We rely on nonprofits when for-profit firms can't (or won't) do the job. If vulnerable populations can't pay for what they need, nonprofits serve them. If problems fester because the solutions aren't profitable, nonprofits step in. Whatever your passion may be—advocacy, the arts, education, the environment, health care, humanitarian aid, research, religion, or almost anything else—there are nonprofits that share your goals and values.

"If you can't find it, found it," said Father Richard Gabuzda. As a parish priest, he worried that the Church wasn't focusing enough on spirituality in training young priests. So Father Rich cofounded the Institute for Priestly Formation. To help seminarians "grow in their relationship with God"—and to help them nurture this among parishioners—the Institute runs a nine-week summer program of spiritual instruction, silent contemplation, and prayer. The program began with six seminarians in 1995, jumped to twenty-nine the next year, and now regularly draws 175 participants.

Like Father Rich, Charles Best also was passionate about a cause and launched a new nonprofit to advance it. While teaching history in a public high school in the Bronx, he learned that his school did not have enough money to cover all the supplies he needed.

"So my colleagues and I spent a lot of our own money," he recalled. "During lunch breaks, we would talk about things we wanted our students to have that went beyond what we could afford from our own pockets—a novel we wanted them to read, a field trip we wanted them to take, or a science experiment that needed a pair of microscopes."

Charles dreamed up a new way to provide these valuable experiences to public school students: raising money on the internet. "This was back in 2000," he recalled, "years and years before 'crowdfunding' was a word or a thing." Although Charles was only two years out of college at the time, he took the bold step of launching a new nonprofit, which he called DonorsChoose.

Charles felt so strongly about this idea that he covered the start-up costs himself. "I was living at home with my parents and they were not charging me rent, so I could spare some of my teacher's salary to get this thing off the ground," he recalled. "I used a pencil and paper to draw out what I wanted the web pages to look like, and a programmer who had recently emigrated from Poland was willing to take my pencil-and-paper drawings and turn them into a website for $2,000."

For the first six months, the new nonprofit, DonorsChoose, depended solely on volunteers. A few of his students helped after school. "Then a few friends of mine from high school and college volunteered in their spare hours to help get the organization off the ground," Charles recalled.

Through their creativity and commitment, Charles and his team of volunteers started something remarkable. Two decades later, DonorsChoose was raising $150 million and funding 250,000 classroom projects each year. When Charles passed the torch to a new CEO in 2022 after serving for twenty-one years, 4.5 million donors had funded nearly two million projects. An idea that was born in conversations in a

Bronx faculty lounge was touching the lives of millions of public school children each year.

These examples highlight a fundamental reason why nonprofits are so inspiring. They empower us to dream of ways to make the world better, recruit others, and work together to make it happen. Even a cynic like me melts at this prospect. What can be better than that?

▨ MOTIVATION

Nonprofits are appealing not only in advancing worthy causes but also in bringing out the best in people who work or volunteer there: at nonprofits, the main motivation is the mission, not money.

A nonprofit isn't supposed to make anyone rich. Even when it earns more than it spends, this surplus has to be invested in the mission. This reassures beneficiaries that the nonprofit is less likely to overcharge them. Professionals and volunteers have less incentive to extract a higher profit, since they can't keep it for themselves.

Indeed, employees usually earn less at nonprofits than at for-profit firms, while volunteers work for free. Usually, both groups are there because of their passion for the cause.

This was certainly true of my former boss Ruth Bader Ginsburg. When RBG founded the ACLU Women's Rights Project, the cause was personal. "I became a lawyer in days when women were not wanted by most members of the legal profession," she told the Senate during her confirmation hearings to be the nation's second woman on the U.S. Supreme Court. The discrimination she experienced steeled her resolve to advocate for women's rights.

As one of only nine women in her class at Harvard Law School, RBG was invited to the home of the law school's dean, Erwin Griswold, who asked each of them, "Why are you in law school occupying a seat that could be held by a man?" In my office at Columbia over fifty years later, I asked how she had replied. "People don't usually ask me that," she said with a mischievous smile. "I told him that my husband was studying to be a lawyer, and I wanted to understand his work."

A year ahead of her in law school, RBG's husband, Martin Ginsburg, joined a law firm in New York after graduation. RBG wanted to keep the family together, since Marty had just recovered from cancer and they had a young daughter, Jane. So she asked if she could spend her final year at Columbia while still earning a Harvard degree. Although Harvard had granted similar requests before, they turned her down. "It was your choice to have a child," she recalled them telling her. As a result, RBG got her degree from Columbia.

Yet even though she graduated at the top of her class, RBG struggled to find a job. "I was a triple threat," she joked with me when she was visiting Columbia for her fiftieth law school reunion, "a Jew, a woman, and a mother." Like many law students, she worked at a law firm during the summer before her third year. But unlike the men in her class, she was not offered a permanent position. When I asked whether they gave a reason, she smiled. "Yes," she recalled, "They said, 'Ruth, we already hired a woman.'" Marty, who was with us in my office, then weighed in. "Ruth, you owe them a lot," he laughed. "If not for them, you'd be a partner at a law firm today."

Like RBG, most people who work in nonprofits are following their hearts, committing their talent and energy to causes that inspire them. This is why Judith Browne Dianis leads the Advancement Project, a multi-racial civil rights organization that supports grassroots activity across the nation. Judith was born to be a civil rights activist.

"My first protest was when I was three," she recalled. Her mother and others wanted a traffic light installed at a dangerous intersection. "They sat all of the children down in the middle of this intersection," she recalled. "I remember chanting, 'we want a light, we want a light.'

"I used this skill some years later," she recalled with a wry smile. On a dinner cruise with her parents, she wanted something that was not on the menu. "I started pounding my fork on the table and chanting, 'I want franks and beans, I want franks and beans,'" she remembered.

Her parents were not altogether pleased, but "the waiter eventually went down to the galley and got my franks and beans."

All joking aside, Judith credits her parents for inspiring her commitment to racial justice. "I grew up in a household with a mother who was a community activist, and a father who had been in the segregated army and bore the scars of that," she recalled. "So race was always a conversation in our household." After a brief stint working in finance, she decided to make racial justice her life's work. "It was like coming full circle," she said. "I was put on this earth to do this work, and I feel very blessed that I have found it."

Indeed, many nonprofit professionals walk away from lucrative careers to work for causes they cherish. Eric Goldstein left Paul Weiss, a prominent law firm where he had worked for thirty years, to become CEO of UJA-Federation of NY, which cares for vulnerable populations and strengthens Jewish communities in New York and across the globe. He was serving as a volunteer on UJA's board when the outgoing CEO, John Ruskay, urged him to seek this role. "The question John asked was, 'at this point in your life, what do you most look forward to in your week?'" Eric remembered. "'Is it your legal work? Or is it the communal work? If this is where your heart is now, wouldn't it be wonderful to devote yourself to it?'" After much soul searching, Eric decided to follow his heart.

Sarah Hemminger made a similar choice. Although she has a PhD in biomedical engineering, she opted instead to found and run the Baltimore nonprofit Thread, which connects academically underperforming young people with supportive volunteers. In choosing this path, Sarah was inspired by a childhood experience. When she was eight years old, her father tried to expose corruption at their church. "They ended up shunning our family," she recalled. "People wouldn't speak to me."

Years later, while pursuing her PhD at Johns Hopkins University, Sarah felt a connection with students at nearby Paul Laurence Dunbar High School, despite their differences. "They are exceptional individuals in extraordinarily challenging situations," she observed, "feeling alone and disconnected." Because Sarah herself knew "what it felt like to be disposable and isolated," she wanted "to create a community where everyone can feel seen and known and loved."

This commitment to the mission is a nonprofit's high octane fuel. It spurs professionals and volunteers to work tirelessly and make hard choices for the cause, while reassuring beneficiaries and donors that the nonprofit's goal is not to enrich insiders but to advance the mission.

DIVERSITY

Along with their work and the dedication it inspires, nonprofits have another strength: they play a key role in celebrating and promoting diversity in society. A group that is underrepresented in other institutions, or does not feel at home in them, can launch a new nonprofit, which focuses on their unique needs and values. Since nonprofits are easy to launch, each community can form their own.

This opportunity is especially valuable for people of color, women, the LGBTQ+ community, religious minorities, proponents of unorthodox ideas, and other underrepresented groups. Unlike government agencies, nonprofits do not answer to voters, so their missions don't have to appeal to the average citizen. As long as someone is willing to invest effort and resources, a nonprofit can champion causes that do not (yet) have broad support.

It is no accident that the Civil Rights movement began in churches and advocacy organizations instead of in the government. While elected officials were mostly on the sidelines—wary of alienating the movement's opponents—nonprofits were bringing court cases, organizing sit-ins and marches, and mobilizing bus boycotts. Once these nonprofits succeeded in broadening their base of support, elected officials had "political cover" to join the effort.

The same is true of women's rights, environmentalism, the religious right, LGBTQ+ rights, Black Lives Matter, and other transformative social movements. They all started in nonprofits.

"The unique genius of nonprofits is the opportunity for new people to come forward with new solutions," observed Eric Fingerhut, CEO of the Jewish Federations of North America (JFNA), an umbrella organization representing hundreds of local Jewish federations and independent communities. A veteran of both nonprofits and government, Eric also has served as CEO of Hillel International, which connects students with Jewish life on campus, as well as chancellor of the Ohio Board of Regents and a member of Congress. "If they can find a philanthropic champion," he continued, "they can disrupt the old order and create a whole new reality."

AUTONOMY: EXPERIMENTATION AND SPECIALIZATION

Nonprofits have the independence not only to launch new social movements but also to test new programs and strategies. Compared with government agencies, they have more flexibility to act quickly, take risks, tailor programs to local conditions, and compete with each other.

"The government is not known for moving quickly," noted Amy Barasch, who spent ten years in state and local government before becoming the executive director of Her Justice, which provides legal assistance to women living in poverty.

Government bureaucracies are often sprawling and complex. Typically, a new idea has to be approved by multiple decision makers with different priorities, agendas, and jurisdictions. Inevitably, some promising ideas wither on the vine, while others take months or even years to be approved.

"Nonprofits have agility that the government doesn't have," Amy explained. As long as their professionals and boards believe in an idea and can fund it, nonprofits can dive right in.

"When you are independent, you can move fast," observed Shira Ruderman, Executive Director of the Ruderman Family Foundation, which advocates for the inclusion of people with disabilities as well as other priorities.

This independence also lets nonprofits experiment with "out of the box" ideas. "The unique role that philanthropy can play is that we can take risks," explained Wes Moore, who was elected governor of Maryland in 2022 after serving from 2017 to 2021 as CEO of the Robin Hood Foundation, which alleviates poverty in New York.

Nonprofits can try things the government can't do. For example, during the HIV epidemic in the 1980s, the New York City Department of Health floated a controversial idea. Since drug addicts were infecting each other by sharing needles, why not give them clean needles for free? Yet even though this step could slow the spread of HIV, some voters were outraged. Wouldn't it encourage drug use? Why should taxpayers subsidize this destructive habit?

When this idea stalled in government, the Robin Hood Foundation and other nonprofits stepped in. Their needle exchanges cut the infection rate among addicts from 50 percent to 13 percent. This is a remarkably cost-effective way to save lives. While HIV treatments cost more than $100,000 per patient each year, a clean needle costs less than a dollar.

Eventually, this track record gave the government "cover" to take over. Robin Hood "doesn't fund [needle exchanges] anymore because the government does it," Wes explained.

This is a very effective division of labor: nonprofits test new ideas, the government adopts the ones that work, and nonprofits move on to other experiments.

Nonprofits have the flexibility not just to take risks and innovate but also to cater to particular tastes and needs. Unlike government agencies, which have to serve all comers, nonprofits can specialize, targeting a particular problem or focusing on a specific community. Instead of "one-size-fits-all," they can offer tailored solutions, which are a better fit for the people they serve. "A community-based organization that knows its community members provides better service," observed Eric Goldstein of UJA.

Shouldn't a community center in a small town have different programming than one in an immigrant neighborhood in a big city? Will government officials in the state capital really know what these differences should be? "It's the nature of government that solutions have to be somewhat cookie cutter," explained Amy Barasch of Her Justice. "They're working on a scale that does not allow for a lot of differentiation among individuals."

But this sort of standardization can lead to mistakes, missed opportunities, and heartache. "There are so many well-intentioned people in government," Amy continued, "but if you've never worked on the ground [in the community you are trying to serve], the amount that you don't know you don't know is unbelievable."

While the government is "a couple of steps removed," nonprofits are "tethered closely and tightly to the communities," explained Kristen Clarke, who led the Lawyers' Committee for Civil Rights Under Law, a civil rights organization that enlists the private bar's leadership and resources to combat racial discrimination.

"Not-for-profits have stronger and deeper relationships within the community," noted Kevin Washington of the YMCA. "The cultural aspects of that community are represented in the not-for-profit, so the level of trust in the not-for-profit is much higher than in the government."

Nonprofits also compete with each other, as well as with the government. This competition spurs everyone to raise their game. "It's through new ideas, risk-taking, entrepreneurial activity, and experimentation that some of the greatest ideas were born," observed Jennifer Sampson, CEO of United Way of Metropolitan Dallas, which promotes access to education, income, and health in North Texas.

■ FUNDING

Indeed, there is much to admire about nonprofits. Along with their missions, the idealism of their professionals and volunteers, and their unique ability to promote diversity and innovation, another strength is worth emphasizing: they tap an especially satisfying source of funding—philanthropy—along with generous government subsidies.

Indeed, charitable donations offer a double benefit, improving the lives not only of beneficiaries but also of donors. If a nonprofit is doing its job, donations help its beneficiaries. Soup kitchens feed the hungry, hospitals treat the sick, universities teach students, and the like.

At the same time, donors feel satisfaction in writing a check, knowing that they are supporting a mission they value. Usually, this isn't something they *have* to do; it's something they *want* to do. Granted, if donors are just responding to guilt or social pressure, they may not be excited to give. But the typical motivation is more satisfying: they believe in the cause.

Surely, this is not the way we feel about most expenses. How many of us get the same satisfaction from paying taxes? Or buying gas for our car? Or paying bills? This is another way that nonprofits are different. Many of us really love supporting our favorite causes.

"You can't beat the experience of working with people who both created the wealth and are giving it away," observed Eric Fingerhut of JFNA. "They have a unique sense of joy in doing it that you can just feel, and a commitment to doing it well. I think they get enormous psychic gratification from it."

In contrast, government programs don't usually offer this double benefit. They are supposed to help beneficiaries, to be sure, but the second benefit—satisfaction in funding this work—is less likely.

"Nonprofits build a connection that donors are unlikely to feel to a government program," Eric Fingerhut explained. "You are going to pay your taxes, and there may be certain government programs you like, but you are never going to feel that close sense of responsibility, commitment, and attachment."

This rare feature of philanthropy—the capacity to make both donors and beneficiaries happier—is a good reason to encourage it. Another is that nonprofits take things off the government's plate. When they aid vulnerable populations or tackle problems that the for-profit sector has neglected, the government doesn't have to do it.

To encourage this socially valuable work, the United States and many other nations subsidize nonprofits. But there are different ways to subsidize them. A key question is how involved the government should be in directing the money.

Like a private donor, the government can make a grant, essentially hiring a nonprofit for a specific job. Yet when the government has to sign off on the project, nonprofits are less free to experiment with "out of the box" ideas.

Instead, to incubate novel (or even controversial) ideas, a subsidy needs to be allocated by private decision makers. To encourage responsible choices, they should have "skin in the game." In "matching" grants, for instance, private donors have to commit *their own* funds in order to unlock government money.

The U.S. tax system has two subsidies that essentially function as matching grants, so private individuals—not the government—decide which charities are subsidized. First, donors are allowed to deduct their charitable contributions. So when we give to charity, the government cuts our tax bill, covering a portion of the donation.

Second, nonprofits generally do not pay taxes on profits they earn. To benefit from this subsidy, a nonprofit has to earn a profit. This means it has to bring in more money than it spends. This money comes from either donations or fees (such as tuition, ticket sales, or health insurance coverage). So once again, government dollars flow only when private decision makers—either donors or consumers of the nonprofit's goods and services—are willing to put up their own money.

"Hands-Off" Subsidies for Nonprofit News Organizations

In these two subsidies, government officials can't influence how much a nonprofit receives, regardless of what they think of its work. These "hands-off" subsidies work especially well for initiatives the government should not control. A compelling example is the press. Investigative journalism is essential in a democracy, but it needs to remain free of government influence.

Journalists monitor society's most important institutions, helping voters, consumers, and investors make more informed choices. But unfortunately, the internet has squeezed news budgets, as readers stop paying for content and businesses shift advertising dollars to the web. To fill this gap, the government might want to subsidize this socially valuable monitoring.

But if the government chooses which news organizations to fund, journalists might "pull their punches" when monitoring the government. So how can the government fund the press without compromising its independence? The answer is for news organizations to become nonprofits so they can accept tax-deductible contributions. Again, this subsidy is allocated by donors, not government officials, so journalists won't lose it by criticizing the government.

I helped my friend Gerry Lenfest implement this idea at the *Philadelphia Inquirer* in 2015. Gerry had a longstanding connection to the *Inquirer* and the city it serves. A few years after he graduated from Columbia Law School in 1958, Gerry moved to Philadelphia to work for Walter Annenberg, the *Inquirer's* owner at the time. After running another Annenberg publication, *Seventeen* magazine, as well as the cable division, Gerry decided to go into business for himself, buying two of Annenberg's cable TV stations. Over the next twenty-five years, Gerry built Lenfest Communications into Philadelphia's largest cable company. In 2000, he sold it to Comcast, receiving more than $1 billion for his stake. After the sale, Gerry devoted himself full-time to philanthropy until he passed away in 2018. He and his wife Marguerite donated hundreds of millions of dollars to an impressive range of causes.

Gerry was Columbia Law School's most generous donor, and he became a mentor and close friend. Gerry could cut to the heart of a complicated issue and had a gift for connecting with people and reading a room. He was honest, direct, decent, and utterly understated. Earning a billion dollars did not change him. Gerry and Marguerite still lived in the same home where they had raised their children. They flew coach, and when Gerry came to Columbia, he took the (more economical) regional train from Philadelphia instead of the Acela express. Even when he started walking with a cane, he preferred to ride the subway from Penn Station instead of taking a taxi. Gerry was not interested in creature comforts; he wanted to do good in the world.

Gerry loved Philadelphia and all it had to offer. He chaired the board of the Philadelphia Museum of Art, the Curtis Institute of Music, the Museum of the American Revolution, and much more. When I visited Philadelphia's Jewish museum, I saw Gerry and Marguerite listed as major donors. Knowing that they were Christian, I asked them about this. Gerry explained that they were always interested in supporting worthwhile initiatives in Philadelphia. "Because of that donation," Marguerite added with a wry smile, "a reporter assumed we were Jewish. So we were included in an article criticizing Jewish billionaires like the Lenfests for not giving enough to Jewish causes." No good deed goes unpunished!

Gerry knew that Philadelphia needed its struggling hometown newspaper, so he joined another Philadelphia businessman, Lewis Katz, in buying the *Inquirer*. They weren't looking for a profit. They just wanted to keep the storied institution from closing. Tragically, Mr. Katz died in a plane crash four days after their bid was accepted. When the Katz family withdrew from the deal, Gerry became the sole owner a few days after his eighty-fourth birthday.

Knowing that Gerry wanted a sustainable way to preserve journalism in Philadelphia, I told him about an article I had written, urging news organizations to become nonprofits so they could accept tax-deductible contributions. After reading the article, Gerry called me the next day. "I want to do it," he said.

For the next year, I worked closely with Gerry and a team of talented journalists and lawyers to launch the Lenfest Institute for Journalism, a nonprofit that became the *Inquirer's* parent company. Anyone who values journalism can donate to the Lenfest Institute, which supports investigative reporting at the *Inquirer*, as well as research on reinventing journalism in the digital age. (In the interest of full disclosure, I served for a time on the board of both the Lenfest Institute and the *Inquirer*.) Time will tell whether this experiment succeeds, but it is a vivid example of how nonprofits can do important work that the government cannot—and, indeed, should not—do.

To sum up, nonprofits have extraordinary potential to do good. They pursue inspiring missions, draw strength from the idealism of professionals and volunteers, and build trust by ensuring that profits are reinvested in their mission. Nonprofits have the independence to respond nimbly, to compete with the government and with each other, and to incubate innovative ideas, while tapping subsidies that preserve their autonomy.

Remember:

- A nonprofit's greatest strength is its mission.
- At nonprofits, the mission is a key motivation, which can impel professionals and volunteers to go the extra mile.
- Nonprofits are a powerful way to celebrate and promote diversity, since each community can launch its own nonprofits.
- Nonprofits have the autonomy to promote novel causes and run innovative experiments.
- Donations to nonprofits produce a double benefit. Along with funding goods and services for beneficiaries, they also offer donors the satisfaction of giving.

CHAPTER 3

THE WORST OF TIMES (AND WHAT TO DO ABOUT IT)

Weaknesses of Nonprofits

AS A SENIOR LAWYER at a leading environmental group, Peter Lehner was a bit startled one day when angry protesters chained themselves to his organization's front door. Were they representatives of polluting industries targeted by Peter and his colleagues? Not at all. Actually, they were die-hard environmentalists who were angry because they thought his organization was too moderate. As the old saying goes, "with friends like these…"

"Groups tend to attack others for not being pure enough, or for being too pure, or just for being somewhere else on the spectrum of how aggressive they should be or what tactics they want to use," observed Peter, who runs Earthjustice's Sustainable Food & Farming Program and used to serve as executive director of the Natural Resources Defense Council. "Sometimes I think people do this because it's easier to attack another green group and you can feel very self-righteous, whereas really you should spend your time going after Tyson and Exxon."

Even though passion for the cause is a nonprofit's secret weapon, professionals and volunteers sometimes turn it on each other. "That is a real challenge in the environmental movement," Peter explained, "and in other movements as well."

Infighting is not the only scourge that plagues nonprofits. All too often, they pursue dated missions, rely on flawed strategies, or spend more than they should. In extreme cases, employees and volunteers even steal from the organization or abuse the very people they are supposed to help.

Why do nonprofits let us down? Unfortunately, the strengths emphasized in the last chapter—their missions, idealism, diversity, autonomy to experiment, and appeal to donors—all have dark sides. The same qualities that inspire us can also lead to frustration and heartbreak. This chapter discusses these weaknesses and then previews a strategy for dealing with them, laying the groundwork for the rest of the book.

MISSION AND GOALS

Since nonprofits exist to do good work, their mission and goals usually are their greatest strengths. But not always. Some missions are less compelling than others, while even appealing missions are sometimes pursued the wrong way.

Indeed, some missions are downright offensive. Did you know that there used to be a "World Famous Ku Klux Klan Museum" in South Carolina? It shared space with "the Redneck Shop," which sold racist T-shirts, Klan robes, and neo-Nazi paraphernalia. Fortunately, a Black minister and civil rights advocate, Reverend David Kennedy, managed to shut them down, persuading a Klansman to leave the Klan and transfer ownership of the property to him. "The South cannot rid itself of its past," he told ABC News. "But we could rid ourselves of the Redneck Shop."

While missions are rarely this offensive, some are fairly mundane—and, indeed, a far cry from saving lives or transforming society. For example, some nonprofits host burger-eating competitions or promote an interest in *Star Wars* (I love the movies, but still…).

Even when the mission is compelling, a nonprofit might still pursue it the wrong way. For instance, the Barnes Foundation has one of the finest art collections in the world. But for decades, it was getting only 1,200 visitors per week, when it should have attracted five times that number. The problem was that Albert Barnes's will required the collection to be displayed in his suburban Philadelphia home, where zoning restrictions severely limited the number of visitors. There also wasn't enough cash on hand to maintain and secure the priceless collection, since Barnes had required the endowment to be invested in low-yield savings bonds.

How do we know that the Barnes collection should have drawn five times as many visitors? Well, that's exactly what happened when a court allowed the collection to move downtown. By the way, one of the key funders of this move was Gerry Lenfest, my friend from the *Philadelphia Inquirer*.

The Barnes Foundation was hardly alone in pursuing a worthy idea the wrong way. It's an old story. Can you think of a house of worship that has let its congregation dwindle? Or a grant-making foundation that applies quirky or misguided criteria? Or an advocacy organization that insists on going to court—doing what it has always done—even when media campaigns or grassroots activism would be more effective?

Unfortunately, "good intentions can all too easily lead to bad outcomes," observed William MacAskill, a philosophy professor at the University of Oxford, in his book, *Doing Good Better*. In response, he and others champion a way of thinking called "effective altruism." "The challenge for us is this," he explained. "How can we ensure that, when we try to help others, we do so as effectively as possible?"

Sadly, not every nonprofit rises to this challenge. So even though some nonprofits pursue inspiring missions in compelling ways, others fall painfully short. Their mission and goals actually are weaknesses, which engender frustration and disappointment.

▮ MOTIVATION

The same is true of another strength of nonprofits: passion for the cause. While this commitment can spur professionals and volunteers to go the extra mile, it also can be a weakness, making them overconfident and inflexible. Sadly, this mindset can have tragic consequences: the missions we cherish end up going nowhere, as scarce resources are wasted and precious opportunities are missed.

The Dark Side of Passion for the Cause

How does this happen? Unfortunately, some professionals and boards are more interested in *feeling* good than in *doing* good. Their goal should not be to celebrate worthy intentions but to deliver strong results.

This becomes harder when nonprofits rely on ideologues instead of idealists. These "true believers" are utterly certain—not just about the sanctity of their mission but also about the right way to pursue it. They want everyone to join them on this true path. If they think you are too moderate, they might just chain themselves to your door!

This closed-mindedness not only alienates potential allies but also leads to mediocre results. "When it comes to helping others," William MacAskill observed in *Doing Good Better*, "being unreflective often means being ineffective."

Wanting to be "pure of heart," ideologues often miss important nuances and insist on (overly) simple solutions. When things don't work out, they refuse to see it. They already *know* what to do (or so they think), so they have no use for probing questions about impact and cost-effectiveness, dismissing them as cold-hearted and even a bit insulting. After all, if there is a better way to do things, doesn't that mean they've been doing it wrong all of these years? Unfortunately, this unwillingness to contemplate other possibilities can lead to mediocrity and stagnation.

Sharing in Profits

In short, passion for the cause isn't always helpful in motivating non-profit professionals and boards, and sometimes it's even counterproductive. This is all the more unfortunate because nonprofits can't use an incentive that is common in the for-profit world: a cut of the profits. By law, nonprofits can't offer equity compensation or other profit-based incentives (although bonuses for other accomplishments are okay if structured the right way).

In principle, the bar on sharing in profits is supposed to build trust: if a nonprofit's professionals and board can't keep its profits, they have less reason to inflate prices or skimp on quality. But although these risks are reduced at a nonprofit, they aren't eliminated. There are other self-serving ways to use a nonprofit's cash, including lavish office space, inflated salaries, generous perks, and a light workload.

Unfortunately, these wasteful expenditures become even more tempting when professionals and board members can't share in profits. After all, pushing for efficiency isn't easy. It's no fun to press colleagues and vendors to do better work, replace those who aren't up to the job, and constantly turn down requests for raises, more staff, and the like. Why take these unpleasant steps? In for-profit firms, the answer is money: every dollar of waste comes out of the owners' pockets, so they reward managers and boards for efficiency. But again, this incentive isn't available at nonprofits.

Reputation & Legal Duties

Since sharing in profits isn't legal and commitment to the mission isn't always an effective motivation, what else is there to keep nonprofit professionals and board members on track? For some, burnishing their professional reputations is an important motivator. They do the right thing—not just because it's right—but also because they care about what others think of them. Like their counterparts at for-profit firms, professionals worry about job security, promotions, and raises, while board members want to avoid scandals and high-profile failures on their watch.

But unfortunately, not everyone focuses enough on the impression they make. Although many nonprofit professionals are utterly dedicated, some do the minimum. Their priority is a relaxed work environment, not the cause. They treat the lower pay scale as a license to do only what they enjoy, while neglecting other responsibilities. Lacking any "can-do" spirit, some are like the manager in a *New Yorker* cartoon, whose two outboxes are labeled "can't be done" and "won't be done."

A similar problem can arise with nonprofit board members. Although many are motivated by a boundless commitment to the cause, some serve for the wrong reasons. "Some people see service on not-for-profit boards as being almost honorary for your gift," observed Eric Goldstein of UJA, "and that it doesn't come with the same degree of oversight and probing that you would expect if you were the director of a for-profit company."

Instead of remaining focused on the mission, some board members are distracted by personal agendas. They spend their time sticking up for pet projects or for professionals they've befriended. "It is a problem when friendships play a large role, along with cliquishness and elitism," cautioned Jay Ruderman, president of the Ruderman Family Foundation. Someone who is looking for prestige and friendships—or, for that matter, special access to the nonprofit's services—is less likely to ask hard questions or make painful choices. Why rock the boat?

In principle, there is another motivation for nonprofits and directors to do their jobs: the law. But in fact, the relevant rules usually target misconduct, not mediocrity. Along with not stealing, officers and directors need to put the nonprofit's interests first and take reasonable care in discharging their responsibilities.

But except in extreme cases, the law does not police the quality or efficiency of a nonprofit's work. The attorney general is unlikely to step in just because a nonprofit's programs are out of date or its costs are 15 percent higher than they should be. There is no fiduciary duty to experiment, innovate, and find the most compelling way to advance the mission. Rather, as long as board members attend meetings, stay informed, steer clear of conflicts of interest, and have a reasonable basis for their choices—even ones that turn out badly—the authorities rarely second-guess their decisions.

Competition

So what else can motivate nonprofit professionals and boards? Although legal duties, reputation, and passion for the cause aren't always effective, and a share of the profits isn't available, there is still another motivation in some cases: competition with other nonprofits, whether for beneficiaries or for donations.

For example, competition for students looms large at universities. As a law school dean, I paid close attention to our competitors. Which faculty were they hiring? What new courses and programs were they launching? What were their new buildings like? Our faculty and students were very focused on these details. At least once a week, someone would say to me, "This other school is doing it, so shouldn't we?"

Yet not every nonprofit competes to serve beneficiaries. At a soup kitchen, the staff usually isn't worried about losing business. On the contrary, they are quite happy for other organizations to pitch in, given the urgency of their clients' needs.

Why is the dynamic so different? To be blunt, the answer is money. Law students write very large tuition checks, so they have the same clout as consumers at for-profit firms. In the United States, this is true also at hospitals, which depend heavily on fees from patients (and their insurance plans), as well as at museums and performing arts organizations, which live and die by memberships and ticket sales. However, when beneficiaries can't afford to pay—at soup kitchens, disaster relief organizations, and other humanitarian organizations—there is less financial incentive to compete for their business.

Even so, these nonprofits still vie for donations. Ideally, this competition brings out the best in nonprofits, motivating professionals and boards to deliver better results. Yet this won't always happen.

The key question is whether the most influential donors—usually the ones who give most generously—are well informed and push for the right things. If they do, there is a "race to the top." To impress these donors, a nonprofit's professionals and board members will go the extra mile to deliver results.

But unfortunately, the same healthy pressure doesn't arise when influential donors are moved more by slick marketing pitches than by strong results. Even worse, if these donors have quirky (or even misguided) priorities for the nonprofit, they might push it in the wrong direction.

To sum up, motivating colleagues at nonprofits can be really hard. Unlike a for-profit firm, a nonprofit can't do this by sharing profits. While some professionals and board members are motivated to enhance their reputations or outmatch competitors, the most powerful motivation—passion for the cause—is also the riskiest. When it works, these mission-driven colleagues leave no stone unturned, hunting for better ways to advance the mission. But when it backfires, ideologues embrace misguided practices, while casting aspersions on anyone who questions their orthodoxy.

DIVERSITY

Again, the broader point is that the same qualities that inspire us about nonprofits can also be weaknesses, so we need to figure out how to bring out the best in them. Just as their mission and their ability to motivate the team can be both assets and liabilities, the same is true of their contribution to diversity. On the one hand, nonprofits have a unique ability to celebrate and promote diversity, as chapter 2 emphasized. On the other hand, the same feature of nonprofits that facilitates this role—independence—can be used instead to promote intolerance.

Some nonprofits also face a different diversity issue, which is about their composition instead of their mission: a lack of diversity among their personnel or beneficiaries.

Promoting Bigotry and Intolerance

Sometimes the problem is the nonprofit's mission. For example, although it's hard to think of an organization more hostile to diversity than the Ku Klux Klan, it actually was incorporated as a nonprofit in 1916. The Klan had initially been launched in the 1860s, but the federal government had shut it down, so a preacher named William Joseph Simmons revived it after seeing D.W. Griffith's movie, *The Birth of a Nation.*

Simmons pitched this "new" Klan as a fraternal organization like the Freemasons, which offered friendship and social activities. In seeking nonprofit status, Simmons downplayed the Klan's white supremacist ideology, although the organization was still committed to it. Instead, the Klan claimed to be "a patriotic, secret, social benevolent order" that would conduct "ritual," sell "paraphernalia, regalia, stationery and other materials," and "publish a fraternal magazine."

The Klan raised a lot of money to spread its bigoted message, while its tax-exempt status sheltered this cash from tax. The Klan sold robes, hoods, and other memorabilia, while also collecting dues from its membership, which peaked at four million in 1924.

The Klan's run as a tax-exempt nonprofit lasted for thirty years. In 1944, the I.R.S. challenged its tax-exempt status, and two years later, Georgia revoked its nonprofit charter. "The Klan is not a bona fide fraternal organization," Governor Ellis Arnall said in an order quoted by the *New York Times*, "but exists primarily for the purpose of arousing, fostering, promoting, and effectuating prejudice, hatred and intolerance through the coordinated action of its members."

While the Klan eventually lost its nonprofit status, other intolerant groups continue to be organized as nonprofits and funded with tax-deductible contributions. For example, "90 white supremacist, anti-immigration, anti-Muslim and anti-LGBTQ groups are registered as tax-exempt charities with the IRS," *CBS News* reported in December of 2020. So even as many nonprofits have played a key role in promoting diversity, others have pursued the opposite agenda.

Lack of Diversity Among Professionals and Boards

Fortunately, only a small subset of nonprofits promotes bigotry in these ways. But many nonprofits face a very different diversity challenge: they are not as diverse as the communities they are supposed to serve. This diversity deficit can arise among various groups within the nonprofit, including beneficiaries, service providers, the leadership, or donors.

Of course, the types of diversity that are important at a nonprofit vary with the mission and context. For example, a house of worship serves specific communities of faith, so there are compelling reasons not to include people of other faiths on the board. In contrast, a nonprofit hospital is supposed to care for everyone in the community, so its board (and patients) should be more diverse, reflecting the diversity of all the people the hospital is meant to treat.

Why do some nonprofits fall short on diversity? In some cases, the problem is bias—conscious or otherwise—but in others it's more complicated. Because nonprofits have a lot of autonomy—again, a quality that is both a strength and a weakness—their professionals and volunteers often have a lot of discretion in recruiting colleagues and successors, as well as in reaching out to (and selecting) beneficiaries. At some organizations, the relevant decisionmakers end up focusing disproportionately on people who share their backgrounds, experiences, and views.

For example, when board members recruit new donors—and, eventually, add some of them to the board—who is on their list? They often ask people they already know, who typically have similar backgrounds, such as colleagues from work, neighbors, relatives, members of their congregations or clubs, and friends from school. In limiting the search, some board members might be motivated by bias, but many are just looking to save time. It's easier to find and vet a friend or acquaintance. Yet by cutting corners in this way, they fail to tap a more diverse pool.

A parallel dynamic can play out with a nonprofit's beneficiaries. For instance, when a school recruits new students, current students can be exceedingly effective partners in this effort. But again, current students might be more likely to know (or more persuasive in appealing to) recruits who share their backgrounds, attitudes, and interests.

To sum up, the track record of nonprofits on diversity is uneven. Some champion tolerance and pluralism, while others stoke bigotry and hate. Likewise, some nonprofits mobilize people of different backgrounds—uniting them behind the banner of their mission—while others have much more homogenous ranks. In many ways, nonprofits have the independence to follow either path.

█ AUTONOMY: MISMANAGEMENT AND WASTE

Just as diversity can be either a strength or a weakness of nonprofits—like their missions and their reliance on idealism as motivation—the same is true of another singular feature of nonprofits: their independence in deciding which programs to run and how to run them. Unfortunately, this autonomy offers the freedom not only to innovate, as chapter 2 emphasized, but also to make self-interested and unwise choices.

Admittedly, people also make misguided choices at for-profit firms, but this is an even bigger problem at nonprofits for a fundamental reason: performance is harder to measure. After all, if we can't tell how effective a nonprofit is, how can we know whether its professionals and board are doing their jobs? This lack of transparency gives nonprofits autonomy "on steroids." Some use it to run pathbreaking experiments, as chapter 2 showed. But others misuse it, offering mediocre programs, wasting money, and refusing to change—unless, of course, we take the right steps to head off these heartbreaking results.

Challenges in Measuring Performance

Managing nonprofits is especially difficult because their performance is hard to measure. This is a challenge even at well-run nonprofits. They have to work harder to figure out the best way to advance their missions.

"In the for-profit world, the bottom line is the bottom line," observed Jay Ruderman of the Ruderman Family Foundation. "In the nonprofit world, there is no real bottom line. People will talk about benchmarks and measurements and so forth, but there's no real bottom line. You're trying to do well, and there are many different ways of accomplishing that."

So which alternative should we pick? In for-profit firms, the answer is straightforward: they should go with the most profitable option. "Capitalists don't care if they earn a dollar's worth of profits by selling potato chips or computer chips," Michael Weinstein and Ralph Bradburd have observed in *The Robin Hood Rules for Smart Giving*. "Profit is profit."

Yet when nonprofits weigh different alternatives, they can't base these choices on profitability, since a critical function of nonprofits is to provide goods and services that aren't profitable. Some nonprofits serve customers who lack the means to pay. Others step in when there is no practical way to charge for the relevant good or service. For example, when a nonprofit reduces pollution or defends religious freedom, it can't provide this service only to paying customers. Inevitably, its efforts also benefit people who don't help foot the bill. As a result, the social value of a program can't be measured by the fees it generates.

The same is true of fundraising totals. The willingness of donors to contribute is a strong signal when they make a fully informed judgment about the nonprofit's work, but not when they merely respond to a glitzy fundraising pitch.

"In private companies, the job is to grow," observed Wes Moore, governor of Maryland and former CEO of the Robin Hood Foundation. But in nonprofits, "the metric we should be determining is not 'is an organization getting bigger?' but 'is a problem getting smaller?'"

Yet this "social return" is much harder to track than profits. How much good does a soup kitchen do? What about a church, hospital, or university? There is no uniform way to measure this, and thus to compare the value of different missions. As Albert Einstein supposedly said, "Not everything that counts can be counted, and not everything that can be counted counts."

Likewise, assuming a nonprofit has the right mission, it still faces perplexing questions about how to pursue it. For example, in helping vulnerable populations, should they focus on U.S. inner cities, Moldova, or Sub-Saharan Africa?

Fortunately, these comparisons become easier as the scope of the inquiry narrows. For example, figuring out the best way to feed hungry people in Moldova is easier than deciding whether to feed hungry people or treat a disease. When the comparisons are more focused, nonprofits can analyze the cost and impact of various alternatives, using metrics tailored to their mission. For example, is the nonprofit serving only the neediest clients? How should it evaluate need? How much food should it provide? Should it deliver the food or rely on clients to get it themselves? By running the numbers on various alternatives, a nonprofit can find ways to do more good with a fixed budget.

But even these focused comparisons can still be daunting. For example, what if the neediest clients are in remote areas, so serving them is more expensive? Is it better to feed 10,000 needy people in a big city or 7,000 even needier people in the countryside? A for-profit firm would simply pick the more profitable market, but what should the nonprofit do?

"It would be most useful—indeed the holy grail of impact measurement—if we could develop a set of standard, universal metrics that would allow us to make true apples-to-apples comparisons between different kinds of organizations and different scales of initiatives...." Raj Kumar observed in *The Business of Changing the World*. "I called a standard, universal metric the holy grail for a reason. We're not going to find it."

In short, picking the most worthwhile goals and strategies is difficult at even the best nonprofits. Social value is hard to measure—indeed, much harder than profitability—so even capable and committed professionals and boards struggle with these choices.

Measurement Challenges: "Cover" for Mismanagement

But the truth is, not everyone is capable and committed. This isn't pleasant to say, but it's true. So what happens when professionals and board members are just out for themselves? Or they mean well but aren't especially talented? How are they affected by the difficulties in measuring a nonprofit's performance?

The answer is sobering: unfortunately, these measurement challenges give underachievers more latitude. After all, since it's hard to figure out the *best* way for nonprofits to advance their mission, it's also hard to know when someone has chosen the *wrong* way. So ironically, measurement challenges at nonprofits make life *harder* for high achievers (who have to work harder to figure out what works) but *easier* for slackers (who are less likely to be held accountable).

This brings us to a central theme in this book: rooting out mismanagement is especially hard at nonprofits—arguably, even harder than at for-profit firms—because challenges in measuring progress can provide "cover" for dysfunctional behavior. Specifically, four types of shortcomings are harder to police at nonprofits: self-interested choices, mediocrity, conflict, and inertia. Let's consider each of these problems in turn.

Self-Interested Choices

Human nature being what it is, the temptation to make self-interested choices is everywhere. We find it not just in the for-profit sector and government but also in nonprofits. But these choices are often especially well hidden at nonprofits: instead of reducing profits, they keep nonprofits from advancing their missions as effectively—something that can be hard to see, and even harder to prove.

To illustrate this point, imagine that an organization—which could be either a for-profit firm or a nonprofit—needs to eliminate one of its two product lines. Since one requires extra work for the organization's professionals, let's call it "hard" and the other "easy." To lighten their workload, self-interested managers want to shut down "hard." But instead of admitting the real reason, they call this "a strategic pivot that lets us focus on our core strengths." You serve on the board of directors, and they ask you to sign off on this new direction.

If the organization is a for-profit firm, exposing management's self-interested motive is easier. The magic words are, "Which product line is more profitable?" If the managers answer (perhaps a bit sheepishly) that "hard" offers a higher return, you are instantly on your guard. Maybe management is right, but maybe they are just being lazy. Now you know that you have to learn more about their plan. You may need to stop it.

But if the organization is a nonprofit, you can't just ask which product line is more profitable. Instead, you want to know which advances the mission more effectively. But there usually isn't a "quick and dirty" way to tell. While you could figure this out by digging into the details, a deep dive isn't practical for every issue. So how do you know when to look more carefully? Facing this ambiguity, you are more likely to defer to management.

To be clear, spotting self-interested choices can be hard not just for boards, but for everyone at nonprofits. For example, funders can't always tell whether their donations are put to good use, while professionals and board members wonder about their colleagues' requests and suggestions. "Hmm...," they think. "They are making a good argument, but what they propose is good for them personally. Can I trust the case they are making?"

Mediocrity

Even when managers and board members *want* to put the organization's interests first, they may still do it *ineffectively*. Of course, when mediocrity is easy to observe, nonprofits can root it out as easily as for-profit firms. They should not tolerate missed deadlines, constant mistakes, rudeness, and the like.

Yet a deeper assessment, which considers the value added by a particular employee, is harder at a nonprofit: the question is not just how the employee has affected the nonprofit's results, but whether those results actually are good in the first place. In other words, because a *nonprofit's* success is hard to measure, *an employee's contribution* to that success is all the more difficult to assess.

Ruth Raskas noticed the difference as soon as she left a Fortune 50 company to work at a nonprofit. "There are different types of systems, different types of incentives that change behavior in different ways," she observed.

After spending fifteen years at Anthem, where she was responsible for driving innovation with technology, Ruth became the chief impact and growth officer at Jewish Federations of North America (an umbrella organization for Jewish federations), and then the chief growth officer at UJA (the largest of the federations). "A stark difference was the pathway from idea to execution," she explained. "When you have key performance indicators that you have to hit every year that are driven from the CEO down, which private sector and shareholder accountability demands, it's very clear what you are rewarded for and what you are not rewarded for."

Yet this approach is less common at nonprofits. In evaluating their employees and programs, some are not rigorous enough. "Far too many nonprofits, even large ones, are run as exalted mom-and-pops," observed Eric Goldstein of UJA, "in ways that are a tremendous disservice."

Compared with for-profit firms, efficiency sometimes is less of a priority. "In the private sector, every year you had to cut admin costs," Ruth recalled. "There were times when we were told that this quarter no one is traveling unless it's an emergency situation, and there were clear boundaries around consultants." But at nonprofits, "there can be more of a focus on community and collaboration," Ruth continued, "but less on efficiency."

"Sometimes the feeling is, 'well, as long as the CEO can bring in enough money, we can spend it however we'd like,'" cautioned Jay Ruderman of the Ruderman Family Foundation. "That's a recipe for disaster."

To deliver strong results, nonprofit professionals need a range of skills, including expertise in the mission, as well as the ability to manage colleagues and raise money. Yet talent in one category doesn't necessarily carry over to another. Some world-class physicians lack the management skills to be hospital administrators, while some inspiring priests and brilliant professors are not effective fundraisers.

To be blunt, good intentions aren't enough to get the job done. Colleagues who mean well won't make a *self-interested* choice, but they might still make an *unwise* one. Let's go back to the organization that is shutting down one of its product lines. Its professionals might recommend the wrong one—not because they want to work less hard but because they misjudge which advances the mission more effectively.

With some professionals, the problem is not flawed judgment but an unwillingness to work as a team. "Sometimes people don't share knowledge because that's power. I become indispensable because I'm the only one who knows this," observed Carol Baldwin Moody, the CEO of Legal Momentum, a fifty-year-old women's rights organization. "It's the worst, worst philosophy for anybody to have."

Other nonprofit professionals are impractical or slow to act. "You're passionate, and this passion means you want to talk—for a long time," Carol joked. "But we've got to figure out what we are going to do."

Meetings in the nonprofit sector often aren't just longer but also larger. At for-profit firms, "people would say we have to think about the ROI [return on investment] on everyone's time," Ruth observed. "Do they really need to be at the meeting? What's the utility of that?" But "my sense is that the communal nature of the nonprofit experience, which I've had in a positive way," she continued, "and which encourages collaboration and the feeling of people coming to the table together, sometimes it's at the expense of efficiency."

Just as professionals sometimes have limitations, the same is true of board members. Many are extremely dedicated and insightful, to be sure, but some don't add the same value. "The problem is that many people are put on boards because they can give [money] to the organization," Jay Ruderman noted. "But first and foremost, you need people who are going to help run the organization well and provide oversight to the staff."

When board members are recruited for their philanthropic capacity, they sometimes have only limited expertise about the mission. Many learn "on the job," digging into the details of the work, but not everyone. Even without knowing much about the mission, board members can still give valuable input on financial, legal, and management issues— often drawing on expertise from their "day jobs"—but they are less effective at monitoring the impact and cost-effectiveness of programs.

While these board members are too hands-off, others are too hands-on. "I don't know that there's always an appropriate understanding of the role of the board," Eric Goldstein of UJA observed about some nonprofits his organization funds. The board's job is to provide oversight and make general policy judgments, while leaving day-to-day operations to professionals. Yet some board members "think that they can call up a CEO and insist that the nonprofit should fund this or do this," Eric cautioned. If they try to dictate personnel decisions, Kevin Washington, the CEO of YMCA, reminds them that this is the CEO's job. "If you don't like what's going on here, fire me," he tells them. "But that's my team, and your responsibility is to hire and fire me."

Conflict

Nonprofits sometimes struggle not only to stamp out mismanagement but also to resolve conflicts. Again, this effort is harder at nonprofits because of challenges in measuring progress, which make it harder for each side to persuade the other.

Since festering conflicts can get in the way of the work, Reynold Levy worked hard to build consensus at Lincoln Center for the Performing Arts in New York, where he served as CEO from 2002 to 2013. "Go visit the Harvard rowing team," he joked with colleagues at an especially contentious meeting, which he described in his book, *They Told Me Not to Take That Job*. "What you will find is that eight people are rowing and one is shouting, not the other way around. Can we try that approach?"

A well-run organization resolves disputes amicably, basing decisions on information and analysis, not on politics and personalities. Lines of authority are clear, and the losing side accepts the decision and helps to implement it. The two sides do not become warring factions.

In theory, conflicts might be less likely at nonprofits, since everyone believes in the mission. But in fact, their passion can add fuel to the fire. For better or worse, fights about principle often are more heated and harder to settle than fights about profit. If we think the other side's position is immoral—indeed, an insult to our mission and values—how can we possibly compromise?

Even when colleagues (mostly) agree about what the nonprofit should do, ego and personality clashes can still divide them. They may compete for raises and promotions, as well as for influence and other forms of recognition. Indeed, where there is less money to go around, people may well fight harder for their share, as well as for other rewards. In addition, just because colleagues work or volunteer together doesn't mean they always get along. Like anywhere else, they sometimes grate on each other, have long-simmering grievances, and form their own cliques.

In this charged environment, bitter disagreements can arise about the mission and the best way to advance it. Similar disputes surface at for-profit firms but, again, there's a key difference: at for-profit firms, everyone generally agrees on the goal—maximizing profits—and knows how to measure it. If one side can show that their idea is more profitable, the other side is likely to relent.

But at nonprofits, this sort of clean resolution is harder to come by. Again, nonprofits don't have a single definition of success that everyone accepts. In a dispute, each side can invoke their own definition, which the other side may well reject.

Like the goal, the evidence also is not as definitive as in a for-profit firm. Since performance is harder to measure, it's more difficult to show that one side's preferred approach outperforms the other's. If the evidence is debatable—or, at least, if it's plausible *to say* that it's debatable—why should either side give up? Instead, each feels freer to dismiss the other's evidence, disregarding Senator Daniel Patrick Moynihan's famous warning that "everyone is entitled to his own opinion, but not his own facts."

When someone doesn't like what the evidence shows, the usual playbook is to claim that the mission is not quantifiable—even if it really is—and to invoke experience, tradition, and the nonprofit's values. "Trust me," they say, "I've been doing this a long time, and I'm telling you that this is the way to go." Or "this is the way we've always done it, and it has made us who we are today." Or the old chestnut that "doing this would betray everything we stand for." As any nonprofit veteran will tell you, feelings can run high.

Inertia

They also will tell you that change does not come easily. "There's a mistake you see in nonprofits," observed Bishop Michael Saporito of the Archdiocese of Newark. "Once they figure something out, they think that all they need to do is repeat it—forever." Old initiatives endure, even as new ones are added.

"It's a problem when people have been there for twenty-five years and have been doing the same thing the same way," observed Carol Baldwin Moody, "even though it wasn't so efficient." For example, when she started as CEO, Legal Momentum was depositing checks only once a week on Fridays. Now checks are deposited on the day they are received.

"Bringing professionals along with change can be incredibly diffi-cult," observed Eric Goldstein of UJA, reflecting on some nonprofits his organization funds. "Bringing lay people along with change is really complicated, and they're almost on separate tracks."

Nonprofits are not alone in grappling with inertia. For-profit firms also operate with standard procedures. Too often, they hang onto them even when a new approach is sorely needed. After all, change requires effort and risk.

Yet nonprofits are especially stuck in their ways. One reason is that their leaders sometimes lack the training to implement new approaches effectively, since they usually have more expertise in the mission than in management. "You're not trained about leading an organization," explained Bishop Michael Saporito. "So what do you do? You just fall into the patterns that you see there before you."

The contrast with well-run for-profit firms is notable. Recognizing that innovation requires a range of skills—not just to come up with a good idea but also to implement it—they often deploy different teams for these various functions. "There might be a chief strategy officer or someone else who comes up with the idea, but in many cases that's not the person, or even the team, that implements it," explained Ruth Raskas of UJA. "There's a certain discipline around how projects are driven and how transformation happens, and I don't believe there are as many of those skill sets" at nonprofits.

Along with differences in training and structure, there is another reason why inertia is more endemic at nonprofits: there is less pressure to change. At for-profit firms, even when professionals and boards are personally committed to the status quo—so they want to say, "if it isn't broken, don't fix it"—these arguments ring hollow when profits and the share price are declining. This is clear evidence that things *actually are* broken.

Yet these alarm bells don't ring at nonprofits. While donations may decline and data on the work may be disappointing, some nonprofit leaders are sure to dismiss this evidence. "Donors don't understand what we do," they tell themselves (and anyone else who will listen), "and these studies don't capture the value we add." So they keep doing what they've always done, as long as they have the money to do it. The unspoken practice becomes, "If *we aren't* broke, don't fix it."

Even if objective evidence can't pressure them to change course, what about their commitment to the cause? Again, the idealism of professionals and board members is a mixed blessing.

On the one hand, it can steel them to make painful choices. To convey this point, a wise JDC veteran used to say, "I don't care about JDC at all—and you shouldn't either. I care about JDC's *clients*." If changing or even shutting down a cherished program was the best way to advance the mission, that's what he would do.

On the other hand, others at nonprofits are too wedded—not just to the cause—but to the minutiae of how they've pursued it. When asked why their organization does something a particular way, their answer is some version of, "this is how we've always done it." Blinded by strong convictions, they won't even consider other options. They defend the status quo in stark moral terms, berating alternatives as unworthy and unethical.

Ego also can get in the way. When someone has helped to shape a particular practice, they can take it personally when anyone wants to change it. Fuming at the suggestion that they've gotten it wrong all these years, they fight tooth and nail to keep things as they are.

To sum up, nonprofits have the autonomy not just to experiment but also to stagnate. Compared with for-profit firms, progress at nonprofits is harder to measure, so there is more latitude to make self-interested and unwise choices. Conflicts are more intractable, and change is a harder sell. In short, mismanagement is less visible, so it can persist unchecked for a long time—indeed, until the money runs out.

Funding

Speaking of money, one more feature of nonprofits can be both a blessing and a curse: their reliance on philanthropy. On the bright side, donations offer a double benefit, as chapter 2 emphasized. Along with helping beneficiaries, philanthropy also offers donors a feeling of satisfaction.

But relying on philanthropy has obvious downsides. For one thing, there rarely is enough money. Nonprofits are supposed to take on jobs that aren't financially self-sustaining. For-profit firms won't do this work because beneficiaries can't (or won't) cover its full cost. Instead, either the government or nonprofits have to step in. But unlike the government, which can compel citizens to pay taxes, nonprofits rely on voluntary contributions.

Since nonprofits have a harder time lining up funding, they can't enjoy the same economies of scale. "The government can do things at scale and in moments of crisis that no individual nonprofit or philanthropist can do," observed Eric Fingerhut, the CEO of JFNA, who also has worked in government.

Relying on philanthropy means not just less money but also more effort to get it. To make their case, nonprofits need to recruit fundraisers, mobilize volunteers, host events, deploy social media, and much more. This effort diverts time and money from the mission—a reality that is never entirely satisfying.

Philanthropy also has another downside: donors won't always fund what nonprofits really need. Rent, utility bills, and audit fees are essential, but not glamorous. Yet if donors write checks only for the direct costs of their favorite programs, who will cover the overhead?

Likewise, what if the program donors like to fund is no longer cutting-edge? To avoid disappointing them, professionals might keep running it, even as more promising alternatives go unfunded.

Nonprofits can experiment and innovate only when donors support this ambition and are willing to take risks. Sadly, this isn't always the case. "A venture capitalist expects a start-up to experiment and fail and learn from that failure and improve, but some nonprofit funders are exactly the opposite," observed Asha Curran of GivingTuesday. "They give a grant to do a very prescribed set of activities that leads to a very prescribed set of outcomes and outputs and everything has to hew very closely to that line and not fail or the grant might not be renewed."

For philanthropy to be effective, a nonprofit's donors and professionals need to be on the same page. When they are aligned, the nonprofit (hopefully) can deliver powerful results, which are a source of satisfaction to the donor. But when professionals take gifts for things they don't really want (or know how) to do, the results are likely to fall short.

The bottom line, then, is that nonprofits' strengths and weaknesses in attracting resources both flow from the same source: their funding is voluntary. This method of financing is satisfying for donors but challenging for nonprofits.

Again, this is part of a broader pattern: the strengths and weaknesses of nonprofits are often two sides of the same coin. While there is nothing better than an inspiring mission, not all missions are inspiring. Passion for the mission can energize professionals and boards, but it also can breed rigidity and infighting. Some nonprofits are paragons of diversity, while others are parochial and insular. Some innovate and experiment, while others just keep doing what they've always done, tolerating subpar results. For all of these reasons, nonprofits can be both exhilarating and frustrating, so hours spent there can feel like "the best and worst of times."

TWO SECRETS OF NONPROFIT SUCCESS: FIGURE OUT WHAT TO DO AND GET EVERYONE ON BOARD

So how can nonprofits capitalize on their unique strengths while also shoring up their weaknesses? The essential message of this book is that nonprofits need to do two things really well: first, they have to figure out the best way to advance their mission; second, they need to "sell" this strategy. To be clear, they have to do both of these jobs at the same time.

But how can nonprofits come up with the right strategy? How can they get "buy-in" for it? The answer is the "Six Ps," which are explained in the next six chapters:

- **Plan**: Run a rigorous planning process.
- **Persevere**: Line up internal support.
- **Prioritize**: Set priorities with "the three questions."
- **Pivot**: Experiment and innovate.
- **Publicize**: Share ideas and hold yourself accountable.
- **Partner**: Raise more money by involving donors in the work.

Figuring Out What to Do

How do the "Six Ps" help? Let's start with the first challenge: coming up with the right way to advance the mission. Each of the "Six Ps" contributes to this effort.

In figuring out their strategy, the question nonprofits should ask is not "what did we do before?" but "what should we do now?" As conditions change, they have to decide which needs to address and how to respond. They also need to monitor their progress, so they hold themselves accountable. To do all of this, a nonprofit needs the right planning process, so the first "P" is "plan."

To develop a better plan, nonprofits should tap the right expertise, take account of criticism, and set the right pace. In discussing how to line up internal support, the second "P," "persevere," encourages nonprofits to take these (and other) steps.

In coming up with their strategy, nonprofits need to be selective. It's impossible to do everything. Instead, nonprofits should look for ways to add unique value. The third "P," "prioritize," explains how to identify valuable initiatives that others can't (or won't) do as well.

When the results are disappointing, successful nonprofits do whatever it takes to turn things around. Even when the results are good, they still search for ways to do better. They are obsessed with improving quality and cutting costs. Can they dream up new ways to advance their mission? Or recruit the most talented group of employees? Or deploy technology more effectively? The fourth "P," "pivot," encourages non-profits to experiment and innovate.

Another way to advance the mission is to share ideas, so others can learn from a nonprofit's experience. Sharing detailed information has another advantage as well: accountability. Evaluating a nonprofit's performance is hard, since we can't use simple metrics like profitability and share price, so there is more latitude to make self-interested or unwise choices. But as the old saying goes, "sunlight is the best disinfectant." The fifth "P," "publicize," urges nonprofits to share detailed information about their work with the public. This transparency motivates professionals and board members to deliver better results, and can also empower donors, the media, and other influential groups to monitor the nonprofit's performance more effectively.

Finally, donors can evaluate a nonprofit's effectiveness not only by reviewing information on the website but also by getting personally involved in the work. In explaining how to engage donors, the sixth "P," "partner," recommends a range of ways for them to play a more active role.

Getting Everyone On Board

But again, nonprofits succeed not just by figuring out what to do but also by motivating everyone to do it. The "Six Ps" do "double duty" by also helping nonprofits get this buy-in.

It is not surprising that the "Six Ps" help both to develop the right strategy and to sell it, since these two efforts reinforce each other. On the one hand, when a strategy is effective, it should be easier to sell. Hopefully, everyone recognizes its advantages and wants to help. On the other hand, as we reach out to try to sell the strategy, we get feedback that can help us improve it. For example, skeptics point out weaknesses, which we try to address. In short, figuring out the right thing to do helps us persuade others, while trying to persuade others helps us figure out the right thing to do.

Each of the "Six Ps" helps nonprofits pursue these mutually reinforcing goals. The right planning process—the first "P"—helps not just to come up with the right plan but also to nurture support for it.

Motivating a nonprofit's professionals, volunteers, and board is critical, since they are the ones who do the work. If they don't agree with a new approach, they will do it badly—if, indeed, they do it at all. The second "P," "persevere," is about lining up internal support.

One way to do this is to involve professionals, volunteers, and board members in decisions, so they feel more invested in them. This is true of the next two "P"s, "prioritize" and "pivot." Playing a role in setting priorities and running experiments makes someone more committed to them.

Along with making the case internally, successful nonprofits also need the right pitch to funders. Just as public companies offer detailed disclosure to investors, nonprofits should share granular information with donors, making their case on their website, in the press, and on social media. To reach a diverse array of external audiences, the fifth "P" is "publicize."

Finally, many donors don't just want information; they want to be involved. Ideally, they come to think of a nonprofit's work as *their* work and its problems as *their* problems. This personal connection makes them even more generous. To nurture this feeling, a nonprofit should ask donors for input on strategy and let them choose how their donations are spent. The sixth "P," "partner," explores how to make the cause personal for donors, inspiring them to be even more generous.

To sum up, the "Six Ps" are an effective way to bring out the best in nonprofits. They counter dysfunctions that fester when progress is hard to monitor, professionals and boards are not motivated or accountable, and donors are not engaged. With a combination of rigorous analysis, steadfast advocacy, and transparency, the "Six Ps" empower nonprofits to develop the right strategy and rally support for it.

This path to success at nonprofits is exhilarating, exhausting, and exquisitely difficult. Some failures are inevitable, but the successes are thoroughly satisfying. It means that our nonprofit is bringing a bit more light into a dark and forbidding world.

Remember:

- Some nonprofits pursue missions that are stale or even offensive.
- The commitment of professionals and volunteers to the cause is counterproductive if it makes them dogmatic and inflexible.
- Some nonprofits pursue parochial or even bigoted missions, while others face another diversity challenge: their personnel and beneficiaries are not as diverse as the communities they are supposed to serve.
- Because a nonprofit's performance is hard to track, its professionals and boards have more leeway to make self-interested or misguided decisions.
- Since much of the nonprofit sector's funding is provided voluntarily, there is rarely enough money. In addition, nonprofits have to invest time and effort in fundraising, which diverts resources from the mission.
- To achieve their potential, nonprofits need to succeed at two challenging tasks: first, they have to figure out the right strategy to advance their mission; and, second, they need to generate support for it among professionals, volunteers, and donors.
- The "Six Ps" can help nonprofits accomplish both of these tasks, so they come up with the right strategy and sell it effectively.

CHAPTER 4

PLAN

Run a Rigorous Planning Process

GOING FROM A UNIVERSITY to run a humanitarian organization—one where I had never worked before—was exciting but also pretty daunting. So in the weeks before I started as CEO, I spent a lot of time with people who knew JDC inside out. As an outsider, I wanted to pick their brains. What did they value most about this storied humanitarian organization, which had helped organize the Warsaw Ghetto Uprising, started caring for survivors just weeks after the Holocaust ended, secretly supported Jewish life in places where it was outlawed or under threat, and cared for vulnerable populations in seventy countries across the globe? How could we build on these strengths? What weaknesses did we need to address?

A number of people offered sage advice. One of them was Stanley Rabin, the head of the board. For Stan, JDC's mission was eternal, helping vulnerable populations and strengthening fragile communities around the world. But Stan was adamant that the way we pursued this mission always had to change with the times. A retired CEO of a multinational firm called Commercial Metals, Stan thought JDC should be as rigorous and nimble as a successful business. He wanted us to take a fresh look and make important changes, encouraging me, as an outsider, to bring a new perspective. The message was "Help us to be better at what we do."

In my view, the analysis that Stan recommended is essential at every nonprofit. They all need to figure out what to do and, just as importantly, what *not* to do. As conditions change, is the nonprofit's mission still compelling? Is the nonprofit pursuing it in the most effective way? Programs that once were state of the art may no longer be successful. Needs that once were urgent may fade away, while others become more pressing.

How should nonprofits navigate this ever-changing landscape? The answer is a rigorous planning process, so the first "P" is "plan." Every year, nonprofits should step back to ponder basic questions. What is working? What needs to be fixed? Which initiatives are "must-haves"? Which are just "nice to haves"? What is the best way to staff this evolving mix of work? How should they fund it?

When analyzing these questions, nonprofits should consult widely. Whoever they include in this process is more likely to "buy in" to the new plan. By involving the right people, the process not only clarifies what to do, but also gets the key players on board to do it.

Admittedly, these benefits don't come cheap. For one thing, planning is hard work. "The time I spend on it," some professionals and boards worry, "is time I don't spend with beneficiaries and donors." Planning also can inflame tensions by pressing nonprofits to grapple with divisive issues.

This chapter considers the advantages and disadvantages of a rigorous planning process and then offers a template for an effective process.

BENEFITS OF AN EFFECTIVE PLANNING PROCESS

Why is the right planning process so important? "We've looked at our planning as a blueprint, not only for values, but also for operationalizing what our hopes and dreams might be," observed Ellen Futter, who served as the president of the American Museum of Natural History (AMNH) in New York City for three decades after serving as president of Barnard College for thirteen years.

Indeed, better planning improves results. The right process sets clear priorities, promotes innovation, enhances coordination, builds internal support, and can even raise money. Let's go through these advantages one at a time.

Priorities

Every year, nonprofits should rethink what they do. What new initiatives should they launch? What should remain unchanged? What should they retool or shut down?

This "blank paper exercise" is critically important, urges Henry Timms, CEO of Lincoln Center for the Performing Arts and former CEO of 92NY. "No matter how prestigious the organization, if you and two colleagues and two board members were starting this organization today with the same mission, what would you do?"

To answer this question, the right planning process clarifies priorities. For instance, United Way of Metropolitan Dallas ran a rigorous process to "narrow our focus from more than twenty areas of focus to three—education, financial stability and health," explained CEO Jennifer Sampson. "To support each of those areas, we identified key strategies; set big, bold, measurable goals; and opened the doors wide open for anyone who aligned with these priorities to compete for funding." In short, instead of just "sprinkling goodness across the community," Jennifer recalled, they developed a "very tight strategy accompanied by measurement standards."

This sort of disciplined planning reinforces a key lesson: just because nonprofits have done something before doesn't mean they should keep doing it. A common mistake is to think harder about launching something new than about continuing the status quo, but it's critical to ask whether past choices still make sense. If the mission is no longer relevant, a nonprofit should choose a new one or shut down. If a program has become stale or bloated, it should be fundamentally altered or replaced.

As management guru Jim Collins has observed in his book *Good to Great*, along with a "to-do" list, organizations need a "stop-doing" list. "Do you have the discipline to *do* the right thing," he asks, "and, equally important, to *stop doing* the wrong things?"

Of course, if a nonprofit has made long-term commitments, these changes may need to be gradual. But even then, why not get started? Nonprofits can still develop a plan and set a timetable for the transition.

Even when the mission is compelling and programs run reasonably well, effective planning is still critical. Instead of deciding whether particular programs should continue, the nonprofit should set priorities for its programs, thinking carefully about how much funding each should get.

In setting these priorities, nonprofits should determine how conditions have changed, vet their results, figure out their comparative advantages, and weigh their alternatives. Chapter 6 digs into the details of this analysis in discussing the third "P," "prioritize."

Experiments

Along with setting priorities, a well-run planning process also identifies and vets potential improvements. How can an effective nonprofit do even better?

As Jim Collins has emphasized, moving from "good" to "great" is not easy. There is no crisis to shake things up. On the contrary, if things are already pretty good, it might seem as if there is less to gain and more to lose in making changes.

Yet the right planning process overcomes this inertia, pressing professionals and the board to test new ways to enhance quality, reduce costs, or reach the right beneficiaries. Some experiments are so important that the organization's entire future rides on them. But in most cases, the innovations are more modest, with each step building on the last. "Good-to-great comes about by a cumulative process," Jim Collins has written, "step by step, action by action, decision by decision."

Not all of these experiments succeed. "Some things are a disaster," observed Bishop Michael Saporito of the Archdiocese of Newark, "so you try different things." The key is to be disciplined enough to shutter an unsuccessful effort, learn from it, and move on.

"Failing is part of success," observed Shira Ruderman of the Ruderman Family Foundation. "If you learn from your failing moment, you actually can succeed more."

Over time, this quest for improvement can add enormous value. Chapter 7 offers more details in discussing the fourth "P," "pivot."

Coordination

In addition to setting priorities and running experiments, planning also helps everyone work more effectively as a team. They share information, mobilize the right expertise, coordinate different activities, and develop and share criteria for making decisions.

This sort of coordination is never easy, especially in large nonprofits. "Legacy organizations often are very much grooved in and siloed," observed Eric Goldstein of UJA, "after decades and decades and decades of doing things a certain way." Different departments function like separate organizations.

"Their attitude is, 'just keep out of my way,'" cautioned Bishop Michael. "'This is what I do and this is what you do.'"

When nonprofits are fragmented in this way, the work suffers. One group might face a problem that it doesn't know how to solve, while another group with the right expertise never hears about it. In other cases, multiple groups address the same issue without comparing notes, so they waste time and money "reinventing the wheel." Sometimes they even work at cross purposes.

But with an effective planning process, the right hand knows what the left is doing. Indeed, they even start to help each other. The goal is a "staff that says 'we all have key responsibilities, but we're on the same team working together,'" explained Bishop Michael. By seeking input from different groups, the planning process taps the knowledge and expertise needed to adapt and improve.

At the American Museum of Natural History, for instance, staff members who interact directly with the public saw a problem that others had not noticed: the museum is so large that visitors often get lost— "not only finding the dinosaurs and the very big blue whale," recalled Ellen Futter, who served as the museum's president for thirty years, "but also the shops and the food court." In response, the museum developed an internal GPS system to give directions. The key to this elegant solution was internal communication: one group flagged an issue, so another could address it.

When different groups give input, they also catch mistakes and avoid misunderstandings. By talking through what needs to be done— and, even better, writing it down—nonprofits clarify the strategy, flag potential missteps, and assign the relevant tasks. With the right planning process, no one ever says, "I thought someone else was going to do that." Everyone knows what they are supposed to do.

This sort of coordination is more challenging—and, indeed, even more necessary—when a nonprofit relies on different types of initiatives to advance its mission. At an environmental organization, for instance, winning in court isn't enough. If one harmful practice is banned, industry might adopt another. "We call this the 'whack-a-mole problem,'" observed Peter Lehner, who has held senior management roles at Natural Resources Defense Council (NRDC) and Earthjustice. Or the legislature might disagree with the court and change the law. "You can end up worse off than when you started," he cautioned. So along with litigation, environmental organizations need to lobby the legislature and regulators, educate industry about greener alternatives, and build support among voters and consumers. "What we're discovering," Peter said, "is that you need a lot of different levers to accomplish these changes." To coordinate these moving parts, the "big greens" need an effective planning process.

The same is true in civil rights organizations. At the Advancement Project, for instance, the focus is not just on litigation but also on grassroots advocacy, public education, and lobbying. Along with coordinating different types of work—whether it is communications, research, policy, community organizing, or litigation—the Advancement Project also helps grassroots organizations coordinate with each other. "We bring grassroots groups together to learn from one another and to strategize together to build out national campaigns," explained Judith Browne Dianis, the executive director of the national office. "We consider ourselves movement weavers." Again, coordinating these different strands of work requires effective planning.

So does another type of coordination: using the same criteria when making decisions. The goal is for everyone to analyze issues the same way, even when they make judgments on their own. This is a powerful way for leaders to exert influence. They can't participate in *every* decision, since a lot happens when they aren't in the room. But leaders can still encourage the team to think the way they do, so colleagues make the same choice they would have made.

To do this, leaders should be explicit about their goals and criteria so others can adopt them as well. For example, during his first year as dean of Vagelos College of Physicians & Surgeons (Columbia University's medical school), Lee Goldman constantly repeated the same goal in meetings. "Be indisputably in the top five and arguably the best in everything we do," he would say. "That's our goal. What does it take to get there?" Soon this phrase became a mantra, which others would invoke. Fourteen years later, when Lee concluded his service, colleagues were still quoting this language. "Even in my farewell video," Lee recalled with a smile, "speakers repeated this guiding principle."

Henry Timms used a similar approach as head of 92NY, a storied cultural and community organization on the Upper East Side of Manhattan, which used to be called 92Y. (In the interest of full disclosure, I served on 92NY's board from 2014 to 2019.) Henry's catchphrase was "healthy, joyful, and T-shaped," and "everyone at 92Y understood what I meant," he recalled. "Healthy" meant recovering from the scandal that ended his predecessor's tenure. "Joyful" referred to 92NY's mission of building community. "The 'T' meant we were respecting the past," Henry explained, "while also embracing the future." 92NY would still offer concerts, lecture series, and other traditional programming (the stem of the "T"), while branching out in new directions by distributing content and ideas globally (the top of the "T"). Early in his tenure, when he passed the cubicle of a colleague on the finance team, Henry was pleased to see a post-it with the phrase "Healthy, Joyful, T-shaped" on her computer.

"That's what you're trying to get right," Henry recalled. "You want a shorthand that people understand, explaining what the organization is trying to do."

Skill Sets and Org Charts

With the right planning process, a nonprofit doesn't just coordinate different activities; it also makes sure that its employees and volunteers have the right skill sets, while updating the reporting lines and organizational structure.

This job is never done. Even if the work doesn't change much, there is a constant need to replace colleagues who leave, find new talent, and rethink the division of labor.

These staffing challenges become even more acute when a nonprofit changes focus, scaling back some initiatives and adding others. The skills and structure needed for yesterday's mix of programs may be inadequate tomorrow.

With the right planning process, organizations get out ahead of these problems. "If we deemphasize X and ramp up Y," they ask, "what changes do we need to make in our workforce and org chart?" They may need to retrain some colleagues, hire new ones, let others go, and merge or break up some teams. This clear-eyed analysis, which is common in successful for-profit firms, comes more naturally to some nonprofits than to others.

"I came from a world where we reorganized all the time, in fact, close to every year, and it was normal and expected," said Ruth Raskas, who left the for-profit sector to work at JFNA and then UJA. "It often enabled goal changes or ways that we wanted to shift our model." These changes had implications for staffing. "We would regroup and sometimes people obviously lost their jobs based on that," she continued, "but that was de rigueur, and from what I've seen that is less common" at nonprofits.

Internal Support

Along with clarifying priorities, running experiments, enhancing coordination, and rethinking staffing, a well-run planning process also fosters buy-in. The reason is simple: anyone who helps craft a plan becomes more committed to it.

To promote this buy-in, the process has to be inclusive. Everyone who will play a key role in implementing the plan should give input— not just to share relevant expertise but also to feel more invested in it.

An inclusive process enhances morale. Employees feel more valued and respected, while learning how their work fits into the bigger picture. "It's amazing what we forget to tell our team," noted Amy Barasch of Her Justice. "It's not that you're hiding it, but you're forgetting to tell them." To fix this common mistake, Amy emphasizes "affirmative sharing"—that is, "remembering what people don't know, and telling them."

While sharing information is always important, it is indispensable in a crisis. When there is an urgent need to make sacrifices and change longstanding practices, buy-in is all the more essential. Everyone has to understand the problem, the response, and the reasons why it is better than the alternatives.

This was critical when Columbia Law School navigated the Great Recession of 2008. The worst financial crisis since the Great Depression, it devastated our endowment and stalled our fundraising. We had to slash our budget by millions of dollars, freezing salaries, cutting positions, and economizing in a range of ways. At the same time, students needed more financial aid and faced a much tougher job market.

To be honest, this was one of the hardest challenges I've ever faced. Squeezing more value out of a contracting budget is not fun, but we didn't have a choice. A lot of people were depending on us, and we were determined to get it right.

To rally our faculty and administrators, we gave detailed monthly briefings, sharing granular information about the budget, job market, and other challenges. We would ask, "Do you agree with the approach we are proposing? Is there something else we should consider?" By including them in decisions, we motivated them to go the extra mile for the school.

For example, one way to save money—hiring fewer visiting professors—was possible only if the faculty pitched in: they had to fill gaps in the curriculum so we wouldn't need visitors for these classes. We asked thirty colleagues—one-third of the faculty—to offer classes they preferred not to teach. To their credit, all but one said "yes" on the spot. "Of course, I'll do it," they said. "I know what we are facing and I want to help." What was different about the one who refused? He was on sabbatical in Europe, so he missed the monthly briefings. Once we shared these details, he also agreed.

The right planning process motivates not just professionals but also the board. They are more willing to sign off on an idea—and, indeed, more motivated to invest time and money in it—if they help shape it.

A well-organized process also empowers them to provide more effective oversight. Keeping an eye on things isn't easy, since the board usually knows less about the details of the work than the professionals they oversee. Board members usually aren't experts in the mission, and they don't manage the day-to-day operations. To redress this imbalance, professionals should provide a written analysis, laying out the nonprofit's goals, strategy, and budget for the coming year. In reviewing this material, the board can dig into the details, pose hard questions, and ask for changes.

By enhancing motivation and accountability, good planning also roots out mismanagement. When professionals and the board are explicit about their goals, they are more motivated to achieve them, if only because failure becomes more visible. Self-interested and unwise choices come under greater scrutiny, while disagreements are aired and (hopefully) resolved.

Planning also can change a nonprofit's culture, encouraging everyone to be more analytical and self-critical. While this comes naturally to some professionals and board members, others are viscerally uncomfortable with hard-headed judgments, "mistakenly believing that applying data and rationality to a charitable endeavor robs the act of virtue," explained William MacAskill, a leading proponent of effective altruism, in his book, *Doing Good Better*.

At JDC, data and analysis were more appealing to some than to others. For example, after the board had dug into the numbers in discussing an unusually difficult issue—whether to prioritize one vulnerable population or another—a veteran board member came over to me after the meeting. "No offense," she said, "but this just isn't fun anymore." I knew what she meant. These choices are really hard. After she walked away, another board member congratulated me for leading "the best discussion we've ever had" at JDC. "It's so important to get into the details so we can get it right," she said.

As these contrasting reactions show, devoted supporters of the same nonprofit can have very different expectations and tastes. At the risk of overgeneralizing, there are "analyzers" and "emoters." Analyzers want data, while emoters cherish moving anecdotes. Analyzers focus on results, while emoters value good intentions. Analyzers reexamine assumptions, while emoters go with their gut. (As I am sure you can tell, I am an unabashed analyzer.)

A rigorous planning process is a natural fit for analyzers, but can it appeal to emoters as well? The answer is "yes," as long as they recognize that effective planning helps produce the heartwarming results they cherish. To highlight this value of planning, why not intersperse some emotional anecdotes in the analysis? For example, a planning meeting can start with an inspiring story and then turn to the nitty gritty of data, trade-offs, alternatives, and budgets. By striking this balance, a non-profit can motivate both analyzers and emoters.

At the end of the day, this internal support is critical. Good ideas just gather dust unless professionals, board members, and other volunteers are motivated to implement them. Chapter 5 offers more detail about how to nurture internal support in discussing the second "P," "persevere." The right planning process is a key part of this effort.

Fundraising

Along with this buy-in, nonprofits also need money. "You can't make an argument for experiments, creativity, and exciting new things if you are losing millions of dollars a year," observed Henry Timms of Lincoln Center.

This brings us to still another benefit of effective planning: better fundraising. A successful process clarifies what a nonprofit needs while also helping to make the case for it to donors.

By setting new priorities and estimating costs, good planning creates a "wish list" for fundraising. Once professionals and boards figure out what they want to do in the coming year and how much it will cost, they can work on raising money for each component of their plan.

Rigorous planning prepares them to make a more compelling pitch. Since professionals and board members have already asked *themselves* hard questions, they are ready to answer almost anything a donor raises. Hopefully, the same analysis that persuades them will convince donors as well.

Effective planning helps fundraising in another way as well: it inspires confidence. Sophisticated donors know that nonprofits sometimes waste money, even on the most compelling missions. But donors are reassured when a nonprofit constantly tracks its progress, compares alternatives, and jettisons underperforming initiatives. This thoroughness and discipline can persuade donors to write a bigger check.

"People trusted that we'd steward the money," explained Lee Goldman. During his time as dean, Columbia's medical school raised more than $3 billion in philanthropic support. "The dean's office was overseeing things and would make sure that they got their money's worth. I think that gave people a sense of confidence."

Finally, the right planning process also supplies up-to-date information to fundraisers. Too often, they are the last to know when needs and strategies change. After all, their job is to *sell* the work, not to *do* the work, so they depend on busy colleagues to keep them in the loop. When this doesn't happen—and, in my experience, it often doesn't—fundraisers end up raising money for yesterday's priorities. But this problem is solved when nonprofits periodically produce a new written plan. By poring over this document, fundraisers learn what to sell and how to sell it.

Frequency

What should the planning cycle be? Should this process run every year? Every other year? Every five years?

Since conditions change every year, I prefer an annual cycle. This ensures that everyone is constantly asking hard questions and rethinking their work. Every year, new experiments are launched, the priorities and budget reflect the organization's latest thinking, various initiatives are coordinated, and fundraisers and donors have up-to-date information.

Yet an annual cycle poses a risk as well: if planning becomes too routine, colleagues might not step back and ask fundamental questions. Instead of charting a bold new course, they might just tinker at the margin. To make the planning process more significant—and thus more of an occasion for "out of the box" thinking—a nonprofit can consider a less frequent cycle, such as every three or five years.

The good news is that this doesn't have to be an "either-or" choice. A middle ground is to have an annual process, but to run a more in-depth version of it less frequently, such as every five years. This compromise offers the benefits of an annual process while also encouraging a deeper dive every few years.

To sum up, a successful planning process enables nonprofits to raise more money and do better work, empowering them to revisit priorities, experiment with new approaches, coordinate different strands of work, nurture internal support, and raise more money. In short, effective planning helps bring out the best in nonprofits.

COSTS OF PLANNING

Yet as significant as these benefits are, they don't come cheap. "Nothing in the world is worth having or worth doing," President Theodore Roosevelt once said, "unless it means effort, pain, difficulty." This is certainly true of effective planning. Not only does it require significant time and effort, but it also can increase tensions by calling attention to hard choices.

Time and Effort

Indeed, just asking busy people to take on another responsibility can raise the temperature. At a well-run nonprofit, professionals and boards already are short of time, and planning adds to their workload. To refine their strategy for the coming year, they have to gather data, analyze results, compare alternatives, and search for savings, while also consulting widely, nurturing internal support, resolving disagreements, and putting the key points on paper. This all takes time.

As a result, there is less time for programs and fundraising, a trade-off that troubles some professionals and board members. "When you're busy with what's happening today, you feel like you don't have time to think about tomorrow," Bishop Michael Saporito observed. "So why is he making us do this?"

The answer is that planning is not a *distraction* from programs and fundraising but a key way to *improve* them. "Once we think differently," Bishop Michael explained, "we can do differently." Isn't it worth it to devote 3 percent of our time to ensure that the other 97 percent is well spent?

This payoff is especially high at nonprofits with large budgets and complex operations. For example, JDC runs hundreds of programs in seventy countries throughout the world. Yet every year, the needs and opportunities change. It would be naive to assume that past choices still make sense. Instead, large organizations like JDC need to keep rethinking what they do.

Admittedly, this need usually is less urgent at small nonprofits. For example, when an organization runs only one program, it doesn't have to coordinate different activities or decide which to prioritize. But even at small nonprofits, planning still adds value: every year, they should make sure their work is still relevant while also hunting for better ways to do it. This planning process can be simpler than at large nonprofits, since there is less to analyze and coordinate. So even if the payoff from planning is more modest at small nonprofits, the (lower) costs are still justified.

Of course, whether a nonprofit is large or small, planning adds value only if professionals and boards take it seriously. "I've used strategic planning to drive organizations," observed Ellen Futter, former President of the American Museum of Natural History, who is a vigorous proponent of planning. "But oftentimes, institutions do strategic plans and then promptly file them in the bottom drawer."

Honesty is critical as well. There is no point in offering disingenuous claims or empty platitudes to justify preordained conclusions. Just going through the motions is a waste of time.

Conflict

Along with requiring a lot of time and effort, a rigorous planning process also can heighten tensions at nonprofits. Which needs are most urgent? What alternatives are most effective? How should responsibilities be divided? These questions can spark heated disagreements.

Yet even if these fights are *fought* in the planning process, they aren't *caused* by it. On the contrary, the same disputes also arise at nonprofits with no annual planning process. The root cause is that there are limits to what any organization can do. Inevitably, some people get the priorities and responsibilities they want, while others don't. Scarcity, not planning, is the real source of this tension.

Even so, a planning process can add fuel to the fire. For better or worse, planning focuses attention on trade-offs and disagreements. Indeed, this is what it *is supposed* to do. A nonprofit needs to be explicit about these choices so it can tap the right expertise and information, give everyone a chance to be heard, and hold decision makers accountable. But as valuable as this transparency is, it also has a downside: losers are all the more aware that they've lost. There is no ambiguity to give false hope or to let them save face.

Yet even if this transparency causes some awkwardness in the short run, it builds trust in the long run. As the old saying goes, "honesty is the best policy." When colleagues aren't going to get what they want, keeping this from them is a mistake. They are going to find out eventually, and they will be even angrier if they feel misled. So even though a rigorous planning process makes it harder to hide disappointing news, I actually consider this a good thing.

Like transparency, another advantage of planning—better coordination—is not popular with everyone. Some professionals and volunteers would rather do their own thing. Eager to protect their turf, they don't want to share information or partner with colleagues. Instead, they pursue personal agendas, jockeying for funding, office space, donors, and other scarce resources. They want autonomy, not coordination.

But whether they want it or not, effective coordination is essential. When colleagues don't share information, they miss opportunities to learn from each other. Likewise, when a nonprofit doesn't compare the urgency of different needs or the effectiveness of competing approaches, it can't allocate resources efficiently.

To sum up, even though planning comes at a cost—in time and effort, as well as in friction and hurt feelings—this price is worth paying. Good planning resets priorities, launches experiments, coordinates different initiatives, generates buy-in, and persuades donors. In short, nonprofits do better work and raise more money.

A TEMPLATE FOR A NEW PLANNING PROCESS

How can nonprofits reap these benefits while minimizing the costs of planning? How should they go about launching a better process?

Decision-Making Criteria: The Three Questions

A good place to start is the criteria for allocating resources. At every nonprofit, professionals and board members constantly have to decide what to do, what not to do, and how much to spend on each initiative. Nonprofits should base these choices not on politics or tradition but on the merits. They need clear criteria, which are rooted in the nonprofit's mission.

At a well-run nonprofit, everyone uses the same criteria. Someone who manages a single program should use these standards to allocate resources *within* the program, while the CEO and board should use them to allocate resources *among all* the nonprofit's programs. This way, an organization's mission and values shape all of these choices, regardless of who happens to be responsible for a particular decision.

When nonprofits launch a new planning process, a productive first step is to ask whether they have clear criteria for allocating resources. If they don't, they should develop these standards. If they do, they should consider whether to change them.

Why is this a good way to start? For one thing, decision-making criteria are fundamental. The whole point of a planning process is to decide how to use a nonprofit's scarce resources. The answers shouldn't be pulled out of a hat. They should be grounded in the mission.

Starting with these criteria is also a good way to get buy-in for them—and, indeed, for the new planning process. There is no point in having decision-making criteria if no one actually uses them. To get professionals and board members to apply these criteria, a nonprofit should invite these groups to help shape them.

This was my first step when we launched a new planning process at JDC. At the time, JDC's many global programs operated with a fair measure of independence. Coordinating all of them from the New York headquarters was quite challenging.

For one thing, it was hard to know what to prioritize. JDC targets a host of grave problems, including poverty in the former Soviet Union, stark economic inequality in Israel, terrorism in Western Europe, poverty in Africa and Latin America, the need to revive Jewish communal life in Eastern Europe, and much more. Comparing the urgency of these very different needs is a challenge, as is determining which programs are most effective.

Making these choices is especially hard because JDC's professional team and board are large and geographically dispersed, so getting input and buy-in is logistically difficult. Almost all of JDC's employees work thousands of miles from the New York headquarters and, of course, far from each other as well. The same is true of JDC's board. It had over 180 members while I was CEO, and they hailed from all over the world.

Because coordination is so challenging, JDC has traditionally afforded a far-flung group of senior managers, called "regional directors," meaningful autonomy in running the organization's leading programs. Their portfolios are defined by either geography (Europe, Latin America, and so on) or goals (research, engagement of young adults, and the like).

As a new CEO, I wanted the regional directors to work more closely with headquarters and also with each other. While they still need a measure of independence—if only because an idea that works in Athens doesn't necessarily work in Azerbaijan or Afula—there also are significant upsides in working together. By sharing ideas and information, they can learn from each other and join forces to target common problems, while also helping headquarters and the board to figure out where additional resources do the most good.

How could I encourage more cooperation? I needed to pick my first step carefully. It had to be meaningful so it wouldn't be dismissed as just symbolic. At the same time, it also had to be achievable because an early failure could doom the whole effort.

So we started with JDC's criteria for allocating resources. As a first step, I met individually with each regional director. "Let's do a thought experiment," I said. "Imagine that you want to run two programs, but you have funding for only one. How would you make this choice?" Their responses were thoughtful and nuanced. Although each responded a bit differently, they covered similar ground.

Drawing on these common themes, I took a stab at synthesizing their answers. After sharing this draft with all the regional directors, I convened a Zoom call for us all to discuss them together. "This is a rough effort to summarize the excellent points each of you shared with me," I told the group. "I need your help to improve this document, so let's rewrite it together."

At this meeting, it became clear that I'd picked the right topic. The regional directors really cared about it, so they vigorously debated the issues, offering examples and counterexamples. They also agreed that it would be valuable to have a common approach. Knowing that they would be more committed to criteria they helped to shape, I relied on them to do most of the talking. Aside from posing an occasional question, I just sat and listened.

After that meeting, I rewrote the document, incorporating the consensus that had emerged at our meeting. We then met again so the regional directors could give additional input on the draft. This time, their changes were minor.

After the regional directors signed off on the new decision-making criteria, the next stop was the board. We circulated a draft to the relevant board committees, seeking their input and approval, which they provided enthusiastically.

So just a few weeks after I started as CEO, we had new criteria for allocating resources, which we had developed collectively. These criteria, which chapter 6 discusses in detail, are deceptively simple. Going forward, JDC would ask three questions every year about each JDC program:

- How important is the problem we are trying to solve?
- How effective is our response?
- Are we the right organization to respond?

By rigorously engaging every year with what we started to call "the three questions," JDC avoided the trap, which ensnares many nonprofits, of reflexively doing what we had done before. Instead, we rethought our goals, ran experiments, learned from the results, and fine-tuned our approach.

A "Bottom-Up" Process That Proceeds in Stages

To be effective, a planning process should proceed from the bottom up. To improve the work, the colleagues who actually do it need to weigh in. What is effective? What is getting in the way? What do they need to get better results? What new ideas do they want to test?

Even as the planning process taps the expertise and experience of colleagues with "boots on the ground," it still needs to vet their ideas rigorously. Maybe they have missed something? Or maybe they have their own agendas? No one should get automatic deference, but everyone should have a voice.

Including all the key players also generates buy-in. If a group is going to play an important role in implementing the plan, they need to help shape it. Otherwise, they might not do their best to make it successful.

The emerging plan should then make its way up through the ranks of the nonprofit. When an organization is divided into different departments or groups, each one should prepare a plan, and then the nonprofit's senior managers should vet it. This review has two purposes.

First, the CEO, CFO, and other senior managers should kick the tires on each group's strategy, looking for ways to improve it. They should ask about the urgency of different needs, the effectiveness of particular programs, possible ways to improve them, administrative costs, employee morale and training, capital projects, new fundraising strategies, and much more. When I conduct these reviews, I like to proceed in stages. After reading the draft carefully, I send pages of comments and questions. Colleagues take a few days to reflect on my input, and then we meet to work through the issues.

Second, when senior managers review each department's plan, the goal is not just to help each department do better work but also to weave their department-level plans into an organization-wide budget and plan. This comprehensive plan should be shared with the departments to ensure that it accurately reflects what everyone plans to do.

The board also needs to review this plan. If there are board committees that oversee particular groups, they should give input on the department-level plans. Likewise, committees with organization-wide jurisdiction—and then the board as a whole—should review the organization-wide plan. In reviewing these plans, board members should question premises, ask for more information on particular issues, explore alternatives, and request changes.

When JDC launched a new planning process during my first few weeks as CEO, we took these lessons to heart. Our process was inclusive and thorough—a productive partnership among the regions, headquarters, and the board. By the end of this process, which took several months to complete, JDC's plan for the coming year reflected thoughtful input from a great many people.

Multiple Budgetary Scenarios

When a nonprofit has different departments or groups and each develops a draft plan, it is helpful for them to propose different versions, which vary with their budget. What will they do with a proposed amount? What if this amount is reduced by 10 percent? What will they cut? Alternatively, what if the budget increases by 10 percent? What will they add?

These scenarios press the department or group to be explicit about priorities and to justify them. This transparency makes it easier for the CEO, CFO, and other senior managers, as well as the board, to decide whether they agree. Any debates are about specific choices, not abstractions. If senior management or the board have a different view, they can work with the department or group to make changes.

With multiple scenarios, it is easier to evaluate priorities not only *within* one department but also *among* several departments. Senior managers and the board know what will happen if they shift money from one department to another, since they can see what the first department will cut and the second will add. These comparisons help determine which departments can do the most with extra dollars and which can get by with less.

Over the years, I have always found it really illuminating to ask for multiple budget scenarios, but there is a catch: the scenarios have to be honest. To manipulate the process, a colleague might try to turn the 10 percent cut into a horror story, which is so unappealing that no one will even consider it. "If my budget shrinks," they might say, "I would have no choice but to make deep cuts in the board's favorite programs."

In my experience, colleagues don't try to play this game—if only because they don't want to be stuck actually having to implement this doomsday scenario. But just in case, I sometimes make a joke to remind them that I won't be fooled. "Hey, if I were you, I might be tempted to say that a 10 percent cut would be the end of the world!" I say with a smile. "But I know you guys wouldn't do that."

In asking for multiple scenarios, I also tell colleagues to ignore donor preferences and other "political" constraints. Instead, I want their best judgment about where funds do the most good. This ideal plan won't always be feasible. Maybe we won't be able to sell some aspects of it to donors, beneficiaries, or colleagues. But to come as close as possible to the ideal, we need to know what it is.

Peer Review

A successful planning process not only identifies promising ideas and clarifies trade-offs. It also breaks down silos, so colleagues in different groups share information and work more closely together.

Silos are a perennial problem in large institutions, whether they are nonprofits or for-profit firms. "Verticals are often siloed," observed Ruth Raskas, UJA's chief growth officer.

To be more effective, nonprofits need groups to specialize, but these specialists still need to work together. This challenge is familiar, but it can be hard to fix. To paraphrase what Mark Twain said about the weather, "Everyone talks about it, but no one does anything about it."

Or, at least, anything that actually works. I have doubts about the approach a prominent consulting firm uses: requiring each employee to spend twenty minutes every other week speaking to someone in a different department. The consulting firm assigns these pairings so that, for instance, someone who analyzes data speaks to a colleague in business development one week and someone in human resources the next week. But in my view, these interactions are too random; the payoff isn't obvious or immediate enough. I worry that some colleagues will resent being dragged from their "real" jobs to have a conversation they don't value. "I'm really busy," they might think. "Why are you wasting my time?"

Instead, I recommend adding a step to the planning process, which I call "peer review." Before the department heads send their draft strategy to senior management, they should share it with the head of another group, who offers detailed comments. Senior management assigns a different reviewer every year, so everyone works with each of their peers over time. To avoid any sense of a quid pro quo, if John reviews Jane's plan in a given year, she does not review his plan during that year.

Since the peer reviewers have deep experience in planning programs, they offer insightful advice. Seeing the group's challenges with fresh eyes, they suggest helpful tweaks and "out of the box" ideas.

This exchange of ideas goes both ways, since reviewers also learn from this process. In poring over another division's strategy, they discover promising ideas, which they can use in their own group. Reviewers learn not just what to imitate but also what to avoid. Armed with a deeper understanding of problems the other group is facing, they are more effective in avoiding these problems in their own work. As the old saying goes, "forewarned is forearmed."

At JDC, peer review was a real hit. When regional directors started reviewing each other's plans, this exchange of ideas inspired collaboration outside the planning process. After discovering shared interests, they followed up by forming joint working groups, inviting colleagues from different regions to brainstorm together, exchange information, and develop best practices.

Why was this silo-busting strategy so effective? The key was that it revealed concrete benefits from working together. Regional directors started partnering not because they were *told* to do it but because they *wanted* to do it. That made all the difference.

A Detailed Written Plan

Finally, the planning process should produce not just a budget but also a thorough written plan. Putting the details on paper has a number of advantages.

For one thing, this document is a useful management tool. By sharing it with department heads, senior managers can make sure everyone is on the same page. If there have been misunderstandings, they are caught, allowing everyone to work out their differences. Once this document is finalized, it functions like a contract, so everyone knows what they've agreed to do in the coming year.

This document also becomes a useful guide for the nonprofit's fundraising. What does the organization plan to do that still needs funding? Using the budget and plan, the CFO and fundraisers should work together to keep an evolving list of initiatives that aren't (yet) fully funded so fundraisers know what to "sell."

A detailed plan also empowers the board to provide more meaningful oversight. Poring over the details empowers them to raise issues and ask for changes.

At JDC, we started producing a new version of "JDC's Global Strategy for Programs" every year. This document answered "the three questions" for each of JDC's major programs across the globe, analyzing the importance of the problem, the effectiveness of the response, and JDC's comparative advantages. By explaining what we wanted to achieve and how the pieces all fit together, our annual plan showed that JDC had clear goals, which we justified, and a strategy to achieve them.

This document was so important that I took the time to draft it myself. Admittedly, this was a heavy lift—especially since the plan changed a lot each year—but there was a major payoff: writing the plan helped me master the details of JDC's work. With this knowledge, I was already up to speed when the phone rang about the latest crisis. I also was in a better position to allocate resources, knowing what each region would do with more (or less) money. In addition, I was able to make a stronger case to donors, using data and analysis instead of rhetoric and platitudes. To hold ourselves accountable, we shared this plan with the public, as chapter 8 explains in discussing the fifth "P," "publicize."

Perpetual Motion

A key feature of JDC's new planning process was that it was perpetual: the new cycle began not long after the old one ended. In launching this rigorous process, JDC sent a clear message: year in and year out, we would keep hunting for better ways to advance our mission.

Remember:

- Every year, nonprofits should step back to ponder basic questions. As conditions change, is the mission still compelling? Is the nonprofit pursuing it in the most effective way?
- A well-run planning process clarifies priorities, encourages experiments, and fosters better coordination.
- An inclusive process also builds buy-in, encourages everyone to apply the same decision-making criteria, empowers the board to provide better oversight, and nurtures a more analytical culture.
- The right planning process also enhances fundraising by inspiring confidence in donors and educating fundraisers about what to "sell."
- Admittedly, these benefits aren't free. Not only is planning time-consuming, but it can also inflame tensions by pressing nonprofits to grapple with divisive issues.
- Nonprofits should consider implementing various ideas in their planning process, including explicit decision-making criteria (like "the three questions"), multiple budget scenarios, peer review, and a detailed document explaining the plan.

CHAPTER 5

PERSEVERE

Line Up Internal Support

AS A NEW LAW school dean, I asked a colleague to rethink a part of our curriculum, working with the faculty committee she was chairing. "We can't spend more money on this," I told her, "but let's see if we can get more out of the money we already spend."

A few weeks later, she came back with a recommendation: a major overhaul that would require a much larger budget. A bit surprised, I reminded her that I had asked for budget neutral options.

"But we *should* spend more," she replied. She hadn't agreed with the constraint I'd imposed, so she didn't follow it.

Sadly, her proposal didn't go anywhere, and we had to go back to the drawing board. She and her colleagues were unhappy, and so was I. We all felt (correctly) that our time had been wasted.

How did we end up there? The naive answer is, "my colleague should have listened to me." But the truth is, I should have realized that she didn't accept a key premise of the assignment. Unfortunately, I hadn't asked enough questions to find out. If I had known, I should have worked harder to persuade her. If I couldn't get her on board, I should have asked her to do something else and given this job to another colleague. In my experience, when someone disagrees with what they are asked to do, it doesn't go well.

This failed attempt to implement a modest change illustrates a critically important point: at nonprofits—and, indeed, at all organizations—it's not enough *to know what needs to be done*. We also have *to get everyone to do it*. Being right is fine, but getting the job done is even better. As chapter 4 emphasized, this is why a good planning process adds value not only in formulating an effective plan but also in getting buy-in for it. Even promising initiatives fail if a nonprofit's professionals, volunteers, and board members don't support it. This chapter discusses how to get them on board. Since this job requires determination, patience, restraint, and a thick skin, the second "P" is "persevere."

"There can be a lot of resistance," observed Bishop Michael Saporito of the Archdiocese of Newark. "The idea that 'change is hard' is one of the biggest understatements of the year. If you think it's just going to go over very, very smoothly, it won't."

How can nonprofits nurture internal support for a new idea? As this chapter explains, they need to find the right division of labor between professionals and boards. It's also critical to be proactive and to set the right pace. Even as nonprofits take these steps, they should empower supporters of the new idea, building momentum with each success. They also need to pick their battles wisely and diffuse tensions with professionals, volunteers, and funders who oppose the new approach. But at the end of the day, when nonprofits face a major issue, principle—not politics—should be their guide.

STAY IN YOUR LANE: DIVIDING LABOR BETWEEN PROFESSIONALS AND BOARDS

To get things done, nonprofits need buy-in from both professionals and board members. Part of getting everyone on board is knowing the right division of labor between these two key groups.

This "requires significant discipline and level setting," explained Eric Goldstein of UJA. "A well-run board knows its boundaries and knows what it's there to do and what it's *not* there to do."

Nonprofits depend on many different people to succeed—professionals and board members, to be sure, and also volunteers, donors, and others. The "Six Ps" in this book are meant for everyone who cares about nonprofits. Each "P" is relevant to both professionals and boards, so much so that I often mention them interchangeably in the other chapters. In planning, for instance, professionals may run the process, but the board must also play a meaningful role. The same goes for the other "P"s. Professionals and board members should join forces in these efforts. Neither group is in this alone.

Even so, professionals and boards are not interchangeable. They play very different roles. Put simply, professionals are responsible for management, while the board is responsible for governance. This means that professionals are supposed to handle the everyday details of running the organization, while board members provide oversight.

This distinction may sound clear in the abstract, but it isn't always easy to apply. What does it mean for the board to provide oversight? How involved are they supposed to be?

To answer that question, let's start with the three key responsibilities that boards typically have at most nonprofits. First, they hire and fire the CEO and set her compensation. The board should make sure they have the right professional leader. They also should set clear expectations, give feedback, and ensure that the CEO has the right incentives.

Second, at most nonprofits, the board has the "power of the purse." Usually, they review the budget and approve major transactions, such as the purchase or renovation of buildings or other significant assets. If the nonprofit has an endowment, the board also oversees the way it is invested.

Third, the board is supposed to make sure the nonprofit complies with the law and uses best practices. Are the financial statements prepared properly? Are internal controls in place? Are potential conflicts of interest vetted properly? Are there effective safeguards against discrimination, harassment, and other misconduct? The board is supposed to make sure the answer is "yes" to these sorts of questions, even as they delegate important details of these efforts to management.

But how much is the board supposed to delegate? In theory, the board's authority is so broad that they can weigh in on almost anything, but this doesn't mean they *should*. For instance, nearly everything a nonprofit does requires an expenditure, so it appears in the budget. But does this mean that the board should choose what brand of coffee is served in the break room? Likewise, since the board has the power to fire the CEO, she has good reason to do what they say. But should they try to tell her whether it's okay to give her assistant a day off?

Obviously not, but the question remains: how should the board use these broad powers? Which decisions should they make? This is the million dollar question. As both a professional and a board member, I've wrestled with it long enough to know that there's no one-size-fits-all answer.

On the one hand, the board obviously must not be "asleep at the switch." They need to make sure the professionals are putting the organization's interests first and constantly hunting for better ways to advance the mission.

On the other hand, the board is there to oversee, not to manage. The CEO and her team—not the board—are supposed to get the details right.

So how should boards and professionals strike this balance? This is too big a question to answer fully here—it deserves a book of its own—but a few points are worth emphasizing.

For one thing, the board usually is better off focusing on general policy instead of particular details. For example, board members should stress the importance of cutting costs, but they usually shouldn't intervene to pick (or veto) specific vendors. The same goes for personnel decisions. Board members should feel free to flag the qualities they look for in an employee generally, but they should be careful about evaluating a specific employee. Do they really have enough information to make this judgment? Instead, the board ordinarily should depend on the CEO to pick and manage her team.

Relatedly, boards should focus more on the decision-making process than on particular decisions. To press professionals to make better choices, the board should ask about the other alternatives they've considered, how they will know whether their plan has succeeded, and what data they have to support their idea. The board's goal should be to kick the tires, not to reinvent the wheel.

In this spirit, although the board and professionals should all be involved in setting priorities, how should they divide the labor? In my view, the board should make sure the nonprofit uses clear decision-making criteria (like the ones at JDC that were introduced in chapter 4). Then, the professionals should apply these criteria and share their analysis, so the board can review it to ensure—not that they agree with every word, but that it is rigorous and reasonable.

When should the board weigh in more forcefully? The answer varies with the circumstances of the nonprofit, as well as the skill sets of the directors. If the professional team is doing a terrific job, why not defer to them? This is all the more true on issues squarely within their expertise.

Yet board members need to get more involved when a nonprofit is struggling. They also have more to offer when the task at hand draws on their unique skills. If a school is sued, a litigator on the board has more relevant expertise than the principal and teachers. Likewise, when a community center is leasing a new building, a real estate professional on the board has valuable experience to offer.

There is no clear playbook for all of this, but I think an analogy is helpful. In ways, the best nonprofit board members are like wise parents of adult children. Just as these parents care deeply about their children, board members are utterly devoted to the nonprofit. But they also know when to stay out of things and when to get involved.

Like parents of adults, board members shouldn't chime in on every minor issue. When asked for advice on these issues, they should give it, but they shouldn't insist that it be followed. "Here's what I think," they should say, "but this is up to you."

Yet their perspective should change fundamentally when the issue is more serious. If there's a risk that their children might make a truly grave mistake, parents shouldn't stand idly by. Even when their children are adults, good parents need to weigh in loudly and forcefully. On major issues, this is what nonprofit board members also should do—indeed, it's what they *need* to do.

STAY FOCUSED

Since nonprofits rely on both their professionals and boards, change requires buy-in from both groups. But buy-in doesn't happen on its own—and, for that matter, neither does change.

To chart a new course, we need to be proactive, not reactive. I learned this the hard way as a law school dean. In the first few weeks, I was overwhelmed by a flood of emails and calls. At first, I felt a sense of accomplishment just responding to them all. When people needed me, I was there! But eventually, I realized that I wasn't doing my job—or, at least, not all of it. Responding to concerns raised by others and dealing with day-to-day challenges is necessary, but not sufficient.

We also need to set a few key goals that we always pursue, even when we are busy with other things. This takes discipline, since life has a way of distracting us. We can't ignore the demands of the moment or the concerns of others, but we also cannot let them dictate our agenda. After all, leaders are supposed to lead.

SET THE RIGHT PACE

A key part of leadership is timing. How fast should a nonprofit move? Some proceed really, really slowly. There is always one more issue to study, one more person to consult, or one more contingency that needs to unfold.

Personally, I find this agonizing, since I am impatient by nature. So when someone says, "Shouldn't we hold off on making a decision and keep our options open?" I think immediately of a joke my law school professor Peter Schuck used to make. "You can die with your options open," he would say. By moving too slowly, nonprofits can miss valuable opportunities.

But moving too quickly is a mistake as well. For one thing, initial judgments about what to do might be off the mark. Nonprofits might target the wrong issue or pick the wrong response.

For Rabbi Aviad Bodner, who has led both the Stanton Street Shul and Congregation Ramath Orah in New York, the first year in a new congregation is "more to observe. You have to see what the needs are," he explains. "I'm not going to come in and say 'this is what I think should happen' because you're gonna fail." A good leader does not "come in knowing what's best for other people," he explains. "You have to know what they want."

Even when nonprofits have figured out what changes to make, they still need to get the implementation right. What steps need to be taken? In what order? How is the labor divided? Are the lines of authority clear? Are the channels of communication open? What might go wrong? What is the backup plan? Thinking through these details takes time, but it is time well spent.

Indeed, launching a new initiative usually takes more time and effort than we expect. I had not yet learned this lesson in my first year as dean. So when I heard an intriguing idea, I was too quick to say, "Let's do it." Before long, I was overextended. To set me straight, the law school's very capable CFO at the time, Ed Moroni, emphasized the old management adage: "If it's not a priority, it's a distraction." It is better to do less but to do it right.

Mindful of this lesson, Bishop Michael Saporito was careful to set a gradual pace when hunting for new ways to energize his parishes in New Jersey. Although he wanted to change the sermons, greeters, music, and much more, he did not try to do everything at once. "It happened slowly and with much time," he said. "It took years to move the needle."

To test a new idea, Bishop Michael did not introduce it at all the parish's weekly masses; instead, he ran a pilot at just one. The Sunday evening mass "was the place where I would roll out these things in an experimental way," he explained, because it "was younger in its demographic," had "a forgiving culture," and attracted people who were new to the parish. Bishop Michael paid close attention to the feedback there. When it was positive, "I always felt like that was a really good indication that something had taken hold," he explained, "and then we expanded things to other masses."

This deliberate pace is helpful not just in testing new ideas and avoiding sloppy implementation but also in lining up support. Since colleagues need to get used to a new idea, it's usually best to start small. This was Ruth Raskas's strategy when she came to JFNA, an umbrella organization representing hundreds of local Jewish federations. How could she encourage these federations to share more data with each other? "We used a POC or proof of concept," she explained. "We deliberately picked small things that we could start to show to people to whet their appetite. I think it was a really effective approach."

Along with giving colleagues time to get accustomed to a new idea, we should tell them about it the right way. Some can reasonably expect to give input, or at least to know about the new approach before it is approved. If it is presented as a "done deal" in a large meeting or mass email, they will not be pleased. When they say, "How could you announce this to everyone before I even knew about it?" what they really mean is "Good luck getting this done without my help."

This sort of mistake is especially costly with people who are already skeptical of an idea. If they think it is being crammed down their throats, their doubts quickly turn into hostility. "Hey, what's the rush?" they think. "Can't we at least talk about this?" Too fast a pace makes them doubly unhappy—not just about the change itself but also about the process for implementing it.

Likewise, a rapid pace is especially likely to irritate veterans who shaped the old way of doing things. Moving in a new direction implies that the old direction—their direction—is somehow inadequate. "Proceeding too quickly could easily...[be] viewed as a repudiation of much of their legacy," observed Reynold Levy, who came from the outside to serve as CEO of a number of nonprofits, including the Robin Hood Foundation, Lincoln Center, the International Rescue Committee, and 92NY.

For all these reasons, moving too fast can be a mistake. This error is even more costly for professionals and board members who are new to an organization. "We might feel like we have to move fast," observed Wes Moore, governor of Maryland and former CEO of Robin Hood, "but first we need to get a sense for the pulse of the organization."

Reynold gives the same advice. "That old adage that if you don't do it in the first six months it won't get done—that's just not true," he said. You can still "pick low-hanging fruit" in the first few months, he explained, "but it takes time to get the institution moving and to change its metabolism."

Before trying to make changes, new professionals and board members need to learn an organization's internal dynamics. What are everyone's strengths and weaknesses? Who is most open about what they really think? Who is more guarded? Who is likely to support a new idea? Who is going to push back? Which colleagues are close friends? Which are constantly at each other's throats?

"Rule number one is don't make a lot of decisions in your first six to nine months because you still don't know the place yet," Wes emphasized. "Anyone can show you whatever face they want to show you for the first six months, but in the seventh month, people start showing who they are."

Pushing for changes on day one also can come across as disrespectful. "There was life before you got there," Reynold cautions. "If you make changes too quickly, and if you convey the feeling that you know too much, you will encounter resistance." Instead, newcomers should find ways to celebrate a nonprofit's traditions even as they try to move away from them. "Institutional growth," Reynold explained, "means respect for memory as well as for the future."

As CEO of JDC, I constantly emphasized the organization's proud tradition of responding to crises and adjusting to new realities. This idea of "a tradition of change" resonated with a lot of professionals and board members, helping to justify new ways of doing things.

But others weren't on board. I was new, after all, and they weren't convinced that I knew what was best for JDC. They worried that I did not value the organization's history and traditions.

The best way to handle this was with patience, holding off on major changes during the first few months and then moving slowly but steadily with one change at a time. "You should change things," a veteran colleague advised, "but you don't have to change everything at once."

I knew he was right, but I didn't have the luxury to wait. My time at JDC was limited. I was there while on a leave from Columbia, since I didn't want to give up my tenured faculty position. (Universities routinely let professors take temporary leaves as a way to encourage public service and enhance their faculty's expertise.) Columbia granted me a two-year leave initially, with an understanding that they would consider extensions later. I didn't know how much time I would get, but I knew the clock was ticking. I hoped for five years, but the university ended up agreeing to only three.

Because time was short, I had to move fast. I worried at the time, and have become convinced in retrospect, that I moved *too* fast. This pace made everything more difficult, causing tension and bruised feelings that I would have preferred to avoid. Indeed, moving too quickly is my main regret about my time at JDC.

Since I knew I was going to stir things up over substance, I did not want to pick fights over symbolism. But unfortunately, I stumbled into this trap anyway when we moved into new offices. In the old space, JDC celebrated its history by displaying photographs of all the board chairs and CEOs from the past one hundred years. The plan was to hang them in the new space as well, but the committee in charge of decorations got distracted by other business. Weeks went by, and the photos were still in boxes. Unfortunately, I didn't notice. Eventually, I learned that some colleagues thought that I personally had nixed the photos to make a statement about moving away from the past. They misread the situation—I actually wanted the photos on the walls—but I should have seen the potential for misunderstanding. Once we got this feedback, we put up the photos right away, but the damage was already done. It was a clumsy mistake.

The lesson here is not about decorating offices, but about showing respect for tradition even as an organization charts a new course. Nonprofits must strike this delicate balance. Otherwise, even the most promising plans won't achieve their potential.

Instead of moving too quickly, nonprofits should follow the wise counsel of my former boss Ruth Bader Ginsburg. "Real change, enduring change," she would say, "happens one step at a time."

RECRUIT ALLIES

Enduring change also requires allies. A single individual—however capable and motivated—cannot turn the ship without help. We all need a crew to help do the work and make the case to others.

"You always have early adopters, and you have to build a team of those early adopters that can help motivate other people," Bishop Michael Saporito recommended. "You have to realize that there will always be people on the other side of the spectrum, for whom change will always be difficult."

One way to recruit and energize allies is to share credit. Colleagues become more invested in a new idea when they think of it as *their* idea. "It is amazing what you can accomplish," President Harry Truman once said, "if you do not care who gets the credit."

Following this advice, leaders should focus on getting results, not on claiming credit. Indeed, because "the buck stops here"—as President

Truman also famously said—leaders inevitably are praised when things go well and blamed when things go badly. The most reliable way for them to burnish their reputations, then, is to motivate colleagues to deliver results.

"I've always said that if I do my job right, I've never had an idea of my own," joked Ellen Futter, former president of the American Museum of Natural History and Barnard College. "It's better to share credit and give away ownership whenever you can."

To recruit allies, leaders also should consult widely, so others feel invested in choices they help to make. Instead of simply giving orders, leaders should ask questions and moderate a discussion, even if they already know what to do. Ideally, colleagues arrive at the same answer—or, for that matter, a better one. If not, leaders can still steer them in their preferred direction.

These consultations offer another benefit as well. Leaders start to learn how each colleague thinks, anticipating who their allies (and critics) will be on particular issues. By empowering like-minded colleagues, leaders can build a team with a common vision.

Allies are especially important when nonprofits make controversial choices. Rabbi Aviad Bodner understood this when his congregation, the Stanton Street Shul, hosted a weekend dedicated to LGBTQ+ outreach, something traditional religious institutions don't always do. Partnering with LGBTQ+ organizations, the synagogue attracted fifty guests who were hosted by members and their families. The congregation wanted "to make a statement about the importance of welcoming the LGBTQ+ community," he explained. "It was beautiful."

To marshal support, Rabbi Bodner consulted widely. "I had a conversation with every single board member about this," he explained. "I also spoke to the membership both in advance and also individually, telling them that this is what we're going to do, that this is our mission. When we went ahead, it wasn't a surprise."

This groundwork turned out to be important when the synagogue planned another weekend of outreach, prompting vociferous criticism from neighboring congregations. "The rabbis of the Lower East Side came together and they made a proclamation that the Stanton Street Shul was not an Orthodox synagogue and they called on us to cancel the event," Rabbi Bodner recalled. "It was very upsetting because our members still live in the broader community and don't want to be alienated from it. There also was a lot of media attention." Even so, the congregation went ahead with the event. Rabbi Bodner had included them in the decision, and they were proud to stand by it.

As things turned out, "for the shul, this was the best thing that ever happened," Rabbi Bodner explained. "It really put us on the map as a progressive Orthodox synagogue. Our numbers grew significantly."

In contrast, things don't go as well when leaders don't get the buy-in they need. I've learned this time and again from painful experience. For example, I was excited about a new fundraising initiative at JDC, but it never got off the ground because I wasn't able to get key colleagues on board. To fund care for our 80,000 impoverished elderly clients in the former Soviet Union, the most effective approach was to bring donors to visit them. Anyone who saw the depth of their poverty was motivated to help. But visiting a village in Ukraine or Belarus was not feasible for most donors. So how could JDC nurture a similar feeling among donors who couldn't travel? The answer was technology. We wanted our website to make donors feel personally connected to the clients they were helping. We had a number of ideas about how to do this.

Yet to implement these ideas, we needed help from colleagues who were in direct touch with our clients. Unfortunately, getting buy-in from these colleagues was a challenge. They were on the other side of the globe, and most of them didn't speak English. In some cases, our request was (literally) lost in translation. In others, they had too much on their plate and didn't want another responsibility.

After months of minimal progress, we gave up on the idea. I was sorry to pull the plug, since I thought this initiative was really promising. But unfortunately, I wasn't able to muster the internal support we needed to get it off the ground.

BUILD MOMENTUM

Marshaling support is not just about finding the right division of labor, staying focused, setting the right pace, and recruiting allies. Professionals and volunteers also need to build momentum, using each success to make the case for their next idea.

This was Reynold Levy's strategy when he became the CEO of Lincoln Center in 2002. He faced a knotty problem: although the performing arts complex needed to be renovated, it was wracked by infighting. "It was one crazy piece of the circus after another with very little comedy, very little dialogue," Reynold quipped. "People were just angry at one another." Unfortunately, the three largest performing arts institutions at Lincoln Center—the Metropolitan Opera, the New York City Ballet, and the New York Philharmonic—all refused to participate in the renovation. Given this internal discord, many thought the project was doomed.

To break this logjam, Reynold formed a coalition of the willing. He started with Lincoln Center's smaller constituents, hoping that early successes with them would persuade the big three to get on board. Reynold formed "the 65th Street working group," which included the Juilliard School, Lincoln Center Theater, the Chamber Music Society of Lincoln Center, Film at Lincoln Center, and the School of American Ballet.

Skeptics did not expect much from this group. They nicknamed it "the Northern Alliance," a reference to an unimpressive coalition of minor Afghan warlords who had helped the United States depose the Taliban a year earlier.

To dispel this skepticism, Reynold and his partners started delivering results. There was "good publicity around the selection of Diller Scofidio + Renfro [as the project's architects], the announcements of gifts, the display of plans, the formation of committees, people feeling listened to and affirmed," Reynold recalled.

The project got a further boost when Lincoln Center recruited a series of impressive new board members, doubling the size of its board from forty to eighty. Word got out that each was committing at least $250,000 per year. "By demonstrating to all the constituents that unprecedented amounts of money could be raised for this cause and that wealthy people were persuaded and cared, we showed what we could bring to the table," Reynold recalled. "For the people who were watching, they'd never seen anything quite like that."

This string of accomplishments did the trick. Before long, all of Lincoln Center's constituents wanted to participate in the renovation project. "Each of those and other steps persuaded people," Reynold recalled. "This time it looks like they're serious." In short, Reynold leveraged the power of momentum. "Accomplishments build on one another," he explained.

Like Reynold, I also won over skeptics by proceeding one step at a time. As a law school dean, I wanted to forge stronger ties between the law and business schools. Fortunately, the dean of the business school, Glenn Hubbard, wanted the same thing. Well, if both deans wanted to do this, couldn't we just give an order and make it happen? Not at all. Not even close.

At most universities, different schools and departments rarely work together, and administrators have little leverage to change this. Since most professors have tenure, they can't be fired and their salaries can't be cut. Ordering them to do something they don't want to do is pointless. They can just say "no"—indeed, they do it all the time.

In forging a partnership between our schools, Glenn and I were starting from scratch. Before then, the two faculties rarely interacted. They didn't share ideas, partner in research, or teach classes together. Indeed, the faculty and students at the two schools hardly knew each other. Although we had a joint degree program, offering both degrees after four years of study, the program essentially enrolled students in two unconnected programs. One year they were in the law school, while the next they were in the business school, and the two experiences did not feel at all integrated.

I wanted to change this for a range of reasons. For one thing, our law faculty has deep expertise in business law, so many of my colleagues shared interests with professors in the business school. They often researched and taught classes on the same issues, so why not brainstorm together and share ideas? A closer partnership would also be valuable to our students. Law students should master the basics of accounting, finance, management, and other business skills. To give useful legal advice, they will need to understand their client's business. In addition, many of our graduates "move over to the business side" to launch start-ups and run businesses.

As a first step, I looked for an ally on the law faculty to help make this case to our colleagues. The friend I approached, a distinguished business law expert, was well positioned to help. Along with his law degree, he has a PhD in economics—the same training as many business school professors. When I asked for his help over lunch, his almost reflexive response was sobering. "Closer ties with the business school," he said, "why would we want that?" He emphasized differences in their approach to research and teaching. If even he was skeptical, I knew we faced an uphill battle.

How can an organization nurture ties among colleagues in different groups? Again, the key is for them to see a benefit in working together—not just for the organization but for themselves personally. Human nature being what it is, self-interest is usually more effective than external pressure in bringing departments together.

To help our colleagues discover shared interests, Glenn and I arranged monthly dinners for law and business school faculty. A professor from one of the schools presented research and then led a discussion of the issue. At these dinners, members of the faculty discovered common interests. Before long, they started teaming up to teach classes and do research together.

Building on this momentum, the law and business schools launched a new joint degree program in which students earn both degrees in three years instead of four. Since three years is the time needed to earn a law degree, students no longer have to invest an additional year to receive a business school degree as well. The program offers a number of jointly listed courses, where law and business school students study together, and finds other ways to integrate the law and business school experiences.

With the generous support of a graduate of both schools, Glenn and I also launched the Richard Paul Richman Center for Business, Law, and Public Policy. This new center, which has co-directors from both schools, serves as an institutional bridge between the schools, promoting joint research, teaching, and events. In short, the two schools have a much closer relationship than ever before, which all started with substantive conversations over dinner.

ENGAGE SKEPTICS

Of course, building momentum through a series of steps won't necessarily persuade everyone. Novel ideas almost always encounter some resistance. While nonprofits should not cave at the first sign of opposition, they also should not ignore the critics. Instead, the right response is to engage them, even when the conversation is unpleasant.

For one thing, the critics could be right. Sometimes a new approach really is misguided. Even when it isn't, skeptics can pinpoint its weaknesses. In many cases, modifications to address their concerns improve the idea.

Yet another reason to engage skeptics is to try to change their minds. If they aren't persuaded at first, it's worth trying again. "Things that some of us see as obvious are not always seen," emphasized Peter Lehner of Earthjustice, which champions environmental causes through litigation and other advocacy. "A lot of people don't have the luxury, the training, or the time to think on this larger scale, so sometimes you have to spell it out."

If the skeptics remain unpersuaded, targeted adjustments in the plan may be warranted to win them over. Reynold Levy understood this when he was negotiating with the Metropolitan Opera and the New York

Philharmonic. How could he persuade them to join Lincoln Center's renovation project? To find out, he dug into the details with them. "At a high level of abstraction, differences are accentuated," Reynold Levy wrote in his book, *They Told Me Not to Take That Job*. "But by moving to facts, to on-the-ground realities, they often can be bridged."

Hammering out this sort of compromise takes patience, creativity, and discipline. There is a "need to achieve consensus, to listen carefully, to constantly evolve your plan, to distinguish between what would be nice and what's really important, to learn the process of give-and-take in negotiation," Reynold recalled, "but perhaps most importantly, to come to the negotiating table with large table stakes."

Indeed, offering something tangible is a compelling way to get skeptics on board. At Lincoln Center, Reynold provided a financial incentive to coax the opera, ballet, and others to renovate their buildings. "We decided early on to match their fundraising," he recalled. "The terms and conditions of the match were liberal and generous and nonrestrictive. We swallowed hard in the interests of comity and worked hard to raise those funds." Lincoln Center committed to raise almost two-thirds of the renovation's $1.2 billion price tag.

Reynold deployed these matches strategically, rewarding good citizenship with especially generous matches. For example, when Lincoln Center Theater agreed to allow a parking lot entrance next door—something that is "not exactly what a world-class theater wants at one of its entryways," as Reynold explained—he agreed to fund a larger share of the Theater's renovation. "The fact that the theater board was so accepting and willing to go along and compromise," Reynold recalled, "made us feel that we needed to say 'thank-you' in some important way."

Sadly, not everyone is this accommodating. To get skeptics on board, nonprofits sometimes need to let them have their way on some issues. Reynold was prepared to do this, at least to a point. "If something was genuinely in the vital interests of a constituent," he said, "Lincoln Center would take that into account and adapt its plan to the maximum extent possible to satisfy that vital interest."

At the same time, Reynold pressed potential partners to be reasonable. "If their interest was peripheral—if it fell into the realm of opinion or second guessing, which is the largest department at Lincoln Center— then we would all agree to drop it," he quipped. "By and large, the constituents would properly answer this question, 'How important is this to you? Because you only get two or three of them. So be sure that this is really important to you. And tell us why.'"

PICK YOUR BATTLES

Yet even the most determined efforts usually don't get *everyone* on board. When some favor a new idea but others oppose it, there is no way to please everyone. If opinion is divided—as, indeed, it often is—should a nonprofit proceed anyway?

On the one hand, throwing in the towel at the first sign of opposition is a mistake. Too often, a new idea is pursued only if everyone is on board. But this gives the status quo an unjustified advantage. If there is strong support for change, why should a small minority be able to stop it? This is a recipe for stagnation.

On the other hand, constant infighting is also costly. If every decision ignites a battle royal, the nonprofit's work is sure to suffer. Instead of focusing on the mission, professionals, volunteers, and funders become preoccupied with the dispute of the day. When they get angry with each other, they don't work as well together. In short, keeping the peace also has real value.

To balance these competing considerations, nonprofit leaders need to pick their battles. In choosing which to wage, they ought to analyze both the merits of the new idea and the political landscape. Is the idea a "must-have" or just a "nice to have?" Is it a major improvement that is central to their vision or just a marginal step with limited upside? Along with the potential benefit on the merits, leaders also need to calculate the political price they will pay. Will they seriously offend a large group of professionals, volunteers, and funders or just mildly irritate a small group?

It also matters *who* is being irritated. In most organizations, some colleagues share their leader's vision, while others constantly disagree, almost reflexively. A politically savvy leader worries less about these two ends of the political spectrum, focusing instead on swing votes in the middle. In the words of the legendary baseball manager, Casey Stengel, "The secret of managing is to keep the five guys who hate you away from the four guys who haven't made up their minds." The key question, then, is how an idea plays with those "who haven't made up their minds."

If an idea would alienate them, pursuing it might not make sense, even if there is a case for it on the merits. We can't get our way on every issue, if only because colleagues become demoralized or impatient if we seem never to listen to them. Over the years, I've learned the value of deferring to others who feel strongly when the alternatives don't seem all that different to me.

But with key priorities, we have to push for what we think is right, even when it means making waves. At JDC, I felt this way about our planning process. It was really important for colleagues to share information and coordinate with each other and with me. But at least at first, some colleagues were reluctant to do this.

With one group, I kept asking for modifications in their planning process, but the head of the group wouldn't change their approach. I made this request several times, in various ways, but nothing changed.

While I prefer not to get tough with colleagues, I felt that I had no choice, so I changed my tone. In a frank conversation, I was candid about my disappointment. Unfortunately, my tough tone angered my colleague. But the good news was that the message was received. The group's planning process changed in exciting ways, and they developed a number of innovations, which generated outstanding results.

To be clear, though, I don't think of this as a situation in which "all's well that ends well." Granted, the conversation achieved a significant goal, but it strained my relationship with someone I liked and respected.

Was this cost worth paying? I raised this question with the executive coach who was advising me. "You asked nicely several times," she said. "Didn't this conversation—tough as it was—finally get results?" When I agreed, she said, "So what's the issue?"

Point well taken. This is what political capital is for. When something is important—as this surely was—we can't worry too much about whether colleagues are happy with us. We need to get the job done. The mission comes first.

But still, I wish I had found a way to achieve my goals without fraying an important relationship. Whenever possible, it's better to get results without making people angry.

CALM THE WATERS

What is the right way to do that? Admittedly, it's impossible to please everyone. At any given time, a nonprofit is sure to disappoint some professionals, volunteers, and funders. How can it keep them from getting angry—or, indeed, from walking away?

Of course, this isn't a concern in the rare case when we *actually want* someone to leave. Admittedly, not every colleague is equally talented and committed, and not every donor is equally generous. Even someone who has these strengths might still have offsetting weaknesses. Some are manipulative, abrasive, or even abusive. Others are inflexible or perennially negative. Still others like to gossip or stir up trouble. When these complicated characters leave, a nonprofit is better off.

But this is the exception, not the rule. In most cases, the goal is to hold on to colleagues and funders, not to drive them away. How can a nonprofit calm the waters so dissenters don't just storm off when they hear disappointing news? The first few days and weeks are critical. As long as they stay involved, there is a chance they will get over their disappointment and rekindle their enthusiasm for the organization. However much they hate the latest new idea, they might fall in love with the next one—but only if they are still around. So how can a nonprofit prevent someone's disappointment on a specific issue from turning into anger and alienation?

To be honest, the best we can do is improve the odds, but there is no foolproof solution. Over the years, I have lost people I did not want to lose. Why is preserving their goodwill so difficult? One reason—indeed, the most commendable reason—is that they care. They are passionate about the nonprofit's work and worry that it is making a grievous error, so they get angry. Sometimes they also feel hurt that their views are not valued. "This is a terrible mistake," they think, "but no one is listening to me!" I myself have felt this way at times, so I understand why emotions run hot.

Fortunately, there are ways to lower the temperature. For one thing, it's always helpful when people who are disappointed by one decision are happy about something else. The good news is that there are always other things going on. Hopefully, if some professionals, volunteers, or funders don't like what's happening on one issue, they are pleased with something else.

In principle, a nonprofit can gin up the offsetting good news by doing something it would not otherwise do. But this is an expensive way to placate dissenters, since the nonprofit has to commit time and resources to something that otherwise was not a priority.

The better course is to please dissenters with something the nonprofit is going to do anyway. To package the bitter with the sweet, a nonprofit leader needs to know what dissenters want, and then manage the timing so something on their wish list happens at roughly the same time as the step they oppose.

Admittedly, this sort of package isn't always possible. Sometimes dissenters don't get their way and there's nothing on the horizon to soften the blow. In these situations, how can a nonprofit keep dissenters from leaving?

For one thing, honesty is critical, even when the truth is painful. Although disagreements can be awkward, ignoring them doesn't make them go away. If dissenters are blindsided—if they expect the organization to endorse their views but it doesn't—they feel betrayed. To spare them from this shock, a nonprofit needs to warn them that they might not get their way.

It also is important to let dissenters make their case. Even if others are not persuaded, at least they took the time to listen. If nothing else, this shows that colleagues take their concerns seriously.

"It takes time just to talk it out and give everybody a chance to be heard," observed Peter Lehner of Earthjustice, who has seen firsthand how passions can run high in the environmental movement. "It takes an enormous amount of time. So much more time than you think, and so you just have to build that into the process."

Admittedly, these delays are not ideal, especially when an issue is urgent. Even when the decision can wait, time spent on these conversations cannot be devoted to other priorities. If every decision requires hours of consultations, fewer things get done. Yet without these conversations, there is a risk that *nothing* gets done. Offended colleagues and funders might undermine the new idea, refusing to help or slow-walking whatever they take on.

Along with being honest and letting the other side make their case, we also need to be careful about the arguments we make. We should do our best to be collegial, offering reasons in a measured way and emphasizing common ground. To quote my former boss, Justice Ruth Bader Ginsburg, "You can disagree without being disagreeable."

Unfortunately, sometimes the other side doesn't heed RBG's advice. They are upset, so they lash out. When someone yells at us, it's really hard not to yell back. I've succumbed to this temptation more than once, and I've always regretted it. I still cringe at some of these memories. It's much better not to take the bait.

Losing our temper is bad enough, but ad hominem attacks are much worse. This is something we should never do. Otherwise, we risk alienating people permanently, so they won't work with us on other issues.

"Conversations can go south quickly when you start ascribing bad personal motives," Peter Lehner observed. "It's not helpful when one side says, 'well, you want this because you're rich,' and the other responds that 'you are being strident because you actually don't have a seat at the table. So you're not being responsible.'"

To preserve a working relationship with the other side, we should focus not just on what we say during the dispute but also on how we end it. When the issue is finally settled, the losing side should learn the bad news the right way. If possible, it should be delivered one-on-one. Although this conversation could be awkward and uncomfortable, the willingness to have it shows respect. Admittedly, this step takes time, but skipping it is likely to make the other side even more bitter.

In delivering this news, we need to show that we still care about them, even if we don't share their opinion. "I value you, I respect you, and I'm so sorry to disappoint you, but this is something we just have to do," we should say. "I wish you were on board because you really matter to us and we need you."

Is this olive branch easy to extend? The honest answer is "not always." At the end of some heated disagreements, I've wanted nothing to do with the other side. But I've tried to get past this feeling, knowing that it is shortsighted. The better course is to patch things up so we can all work together on other issues.

CHANGE THE CULTURE

Finding a way to "disagree without being disagreeable" should be our goal not just in resolving a particular dispute, but also in shaping our nonprofit's culture. At healthy organizations, debates are robust, but the tone is civil. Colleagues are comfortable being honest with each other. As blunt as they are, they are never insulting. They are welcome to say,

"This is a really serious mistake," but they would never say, "You are either dishonest or stupid, so which is it?"

Disputes also don't drag on. Well-run organizations have a clear and accepted method for resolving disagreements, whether through a vote or a chain of command. Once the decision is made, everyone comes together to implement it.

Likewise, there are no warring factions. The same people are not constantly at each other's throats on every decision. Instead, colleagues who disagree on one issue are just as likely to agree on another.

"Instead of infighting, it is better to find strength in differences," Peter Lehner explained. "At every point, try to focus on the issues and the strategies, not the people."

Nurturing this sort of culture is not easy. Veterans of the organization need to model it, while newcomers have to buy into it. Preserving a unique culture was a key priority for Sarah Hemminger, the co-founder and CEO of Thread, which supports students in Baltimore by matching them with up to four volunteers. This "Thread family" does more than "continuously show up for a young person and provide a ride to school or provide tutoring," Sarah explained. Instead, volunteers treat students as friends and equals, "showing deep vulnerability" and "sharing with the young person, 'Hey, I got in a fight with my spouse this morning' or 'I'm having a hard time at work right now.'" Treating students as peers empowers them. "When you know you're very needed and you're helpful," Sarah observed, "you start to change how you feel about yourself."

As part of this effort, Thread's culture encourages staff, as well as volunteers, to be utterly honest but also collegial. "We talk about 'calling a thing a thing,' 'telling the truth with love,' and 'directness with kindness,'" Sarah explained. "This is a direct conflict with the dominant culture, which is all about being polite." During its first six years, Thread was an all-volunteer organization, and this initial cohort of volunteers helped forge this culture.

When Sarah started hiring professional staff, she encountered an unexpected problem. The new hires "weren't willing to say, 'hey, this is all messed up, so we should do this other thing,'" Sarah recalled. "I just assumed when we started bringing on staff that they would engage the same ways volunteers did, but I didn't understand just how deeply the dominant culture is embedded in the workplace. I didn't predict well enough what people would bring in with them when they came on staff."

Sarah knew this was a major problem. "I would have thought that bringing on paid people made things easier, but that actually wasn't true at first," she recalled. "One of the hardest things is making sure that the staff culture is truly reflective of the behavior and norms that have led to really incredible outcomes for our young people."

Sarah came up with a creative solution: hiring Thread alumni. These former students had been mentored in the program, so they were already steeped in the culture and could model it for others.

"We'd be in staff meetings and I'd say something," Sarah recalled, "and they'd say, 'Well, I fundamentally disagree with that. Here's the reason. That's ridiculous. We'll do it this way.'" At first, these blunt interventions were startling to the rest of the staff. "Everyone else would just look kind of like, 'What?'" she recalled with a smile. But pretty soon, other professionals started following their lead. "That really helped a ton," Sarah remembered.

Indeed, the right culture—and, more fundamentally, a determined effort to "disagree without being disagreeable"—can keep dissenters from storming off. By letting them make their case, taking time to explain why their views haven't carried the day, treating them with courtesy and respect, and softening the blow with good news on other issues (when possible), nonprofits often can preserve these important ties.

FOLLOW YOUR CONSCIENCE

The truth is, dealing with disappointed people is part of life at nonprofits. Indeed, critics usually are more vocal than supporters. When people like what's happening, they tend to take things for granted. "Of course the organization is doing what we want," they think. "Why wouldn't it?" Feedback seems unnecessary. Why praise an organization for just doing what it's supposed to do?

But when people are unhappy, they have a lot more to say. Sometimes this feedback is diplomatic and restrained, but sometimes... well, not so much. Ideally, they have spoken to a colleague or friend on the other side of the issue, so they know their view is not self-evident or universal. But in my experience, this sort of communication is not common enough, so the critics' reaction often is some version of, "What in the world is going on? Why are we doing this unimaginably senseless thing?"

This means a nonprofit leader has to devote a lot of time to explaining each side's view to the other and, more generally, to dealing with unhappy professionals, volunteers, and funders. The stream of criticism is constant.

For me, the best way to deal with this criticism is to believe in what I am doing. As long as I think I am right, people can say what they want. I may be frustrated that I haven't gotten through to them. I may worry that I don't have enough support to proceed. I may be sad that people I care about are unhappy or disappointed. But I don't feel guilty. I don't feel as if I am letting down the organization.

But this is exactly how I feel when I go along with something I don't actually believe. In my first few months as a law school dean, I made a few decisions based on political considerations, not the merits. Not surprisingly, some colleagues disagreed with those choices. Their criticism stung all the more because I agreed with it. They were saying what I really thought.

This experience reminded me of something RBG used to tell me and her other law clerks. "Figuring out the politics is hard," she would say. "Just do what you think is right."

This is not to say that we should never compromise or that we need to have our way on every little detail. That would be unreasonable and, indeed, wildly impractical. We would never get anything done.

But on major issues, we need to follow our conscience. Someone is always going to criticize us. When we answer them, we need to believe what we are saying. As long as we are true to ourselves, we can deal with their disappointment and anger. We can even deal with failure, knowing that at least we've tried. We might well pay a price for following our conscience, but the price of *not* following it is higher.

This insight has guided me through many difficult times, including when another school at Columbia invited a very controversial speaker: Mahmoud Ahmadinejad, the president of Iran. He was opposed to equal rights for women, the LGBTQ+ community, and religious minorities. A Holocaust denier who regularly called for the destruction of Israel, Ahmadinejad also was waging a proxy war against the United States in Iraq at the time.

Even so, faculty members at Columbia's School of International and Public Affairs (SIPA) wanted to host him. As part of Columbia's commitment to academic freedom, faculty and students have a great deal of discretion in inviting speakers.

This put Lee Bollinger, the university president at the time (and my boss), in an awkward position. He decided to join the SIPA faculty in extending the invitation, so he could signal support for academic freedom while also playing a personal role in managing this controversial event.

When news of this invitation became public, I received hundreds of angry calls and emails from law school graduates and students. At the same time, others were proud of the invitation, invoking it as a sign of the university's commitment to free speech.

Under pressure to say something, I knew I was in a no-win situation. Whatever I said, I was going to anger one side or the other. So I remembered RBG's advice. I set aside politics and followed my conscience.

In my view, Ahmadinejad was a repugnant and dangerous bigot. I saw no academic value in hosting someone who spreads hateful lies. I worried that inviting him to speak at a great university could afford him undeserved legitimacy.

At the same time, I recognized that this wasn't my choice to make. In a community that is committed to academic freedom, individuals can extend invitations that are unappealing or even offensive to others.

But academic freedom is a two-way street. Just as my colleagues were allowed to extend this invitation, I had the right to criticize it, even though my boss was one of the people (reluctantly) extending it. So I posted a short statement on the law school's website:

> A controversy has developed about the invitation extended to President Mahmoud Ahmadinejad of Iran by the Columbia School of International and Public Affairs. Although Columbia Law School was not involved in arranging this invitation, we have received many inquiries about it.
>
> This event raises deep and complicated issues about how best to express our commitment to intellectual freedom, and to our free way of life. Although we believe in free and open debate at Columbia and should never suppress points of view, we are also committed to academic standards. A high-quality academic discussion depends on intellectual honesty but, unfortunately, Mr. Ahmadinejad has proven himself, time and again, to be uninterested in whether his words are true. Therefore, my personal opinion is that he should not be invited to speak. Mr. Ahmadinejad is a reprehensible and dangerous figure who presides over a repressive regime, is responsible for the death of American soldiers, denies the Holocaust, and calls for the destruction of Israel. It would be deeply regrettable if some misread this invitation as lending prestige or legitimacy to his views.
>
> Our university is a pluralistic place, and I recognize that others within our community take a different view

in good faith, and that they have the right to extend invitations that I personally would not extend. I know that we will learn from each other in discussing the difficult questions prompted by this invitation.

This controversy (and my statement) ended up attracting a lot of attention in the media. While some were enthusiastic about what I said, others were angry. But I was comfortable with this criticism, knowing that I felt strongly about what I'd said.

Meanwhile, the fireworks around the invitation continued. The dean of SIPA, John Coatsworth, appeared on Fox News to defend the invitation, arguing that Columbia should be prepared to host any national leader as long as they were not at war with the United States. Asked whether he would have invited Adolf Hitler before Germany invaded Poland in 1939, Coatsworth replied, "If he were willing to engage in a debate and discussion, and be challenged by Columbia students and faculty, we would certainly invite him." This comment did not persuade the *New York Daily News*, which opined that the "thought of engaging the guiding force of the Third Reich in collegial debate is simply monstrous."

A few days later, President Bollinger introduced President Ahmadinejad's remarks by offering a stinging critique of the Iranian leader. "Mr. President, you exhibit all the signs of a petty and cruel dictator," he said. "You are either brazenly provocative or astonishingly uneducated."

Ahmadinejad responded with a rebuke of his own: "In Iran, tradition requires when you invite a person to be a speaker, we actually respect our students enough to allow them to make their own judgment, and don't think it's necessary before the speech is even given to come in with a series of complaints to provide vaccination to the students and faculty."

Ahmadinejad went on to confirm my observation that intellectual honesty was not his strong suit. For example, when he was asked about discrimination against women in Iran, Ahmadinejad replied that "women in Iran enjoy the highest levels of freedom." Likewise, when challenged about the persecution of the LGBTQ+ community, he responded: "In Iran, we don't have homosexuals, like in your country."

Eventually, the strong feelings surrounding this visit died down. But as with other challenging situations over the years, it left me feeling drained. Indeed, as exhilarating as life can be at nonprofits, it also can be exhausting.

PRESS ON

But we need to keep going. "You have to be prepared to move and have a tough enough stomach," observed Wes Moore, governor of Maryland and former CEO of Robin Hood. "You're going to have bad days, but you're still going to get up tomorrow and make more decisions."

Sometimes we don't get our way, but we have to remember that it's impossible to win every battle. Indeed, if we succeed at everything we try, we aren't aiming high enough.

How should we deal with disappointment? The best advice I've heard comes from Gray Davis, a Columbia Law School graduate who served as governor of California. A few months into his second term, he lost a recall election to Arnold Schwarzenegger, a prominent actor turned politician. Governor Davis reflected on this experience in one of the finest commencement speeches I've ever heard.

"You cannot control what life brings your way," he said. "You can only control *how you react to it.*" It's important to be gracious, stay positive, and try something else. Like the rest of the audience, I also loved Governor Davis's next line. "In my opinion, you haven't really lived," he joked, "until Arnold Schwarzenegger says to *you personally,* 'Hasta la vista, baby.'"

Admittedly, when things don't go our way, it's natural to think about giving up. "Are there disappointments along the way? Sure there are," explained Bishop Michael Saporito. "Any time you've enlightened yourself and you want other people to see it and they can't, at least temporarily, it can be really disappointing. Some days you walk away, thinking 'Why did I even start this? Why? It would be just so much easier if I would have left it alone.'"

So how do we press on? Where do we find the strength? The answer, of course, is the mission. Knowing how important it is, we refuse to give up. "The point is not change for change's sake, but to bring joy to the work," Bishop Michael explained. "Change brings creativity to the mission. It brings hope to me personally to be part of it, and not to be stuck in the way things have always been."

We also draw strength from successes, both large and small. Each encouraging development recharges our batteries, reminding us why we do what we do. "At those times when you feel like you're empty, someone always comes along and tells you how much something we did matters to them, how it has made a difference in their lives," Bishop Michael observed with a smile. "And you think, 'That's why this effort is worth it.' And you pick yourself back up and you say 'I've got to keep going.'"

Of all the challenges in this book, the toughest, at least for me, is nurturing internal support for change. There is almost always pushback. To overcome it, we need to assign the right roles to professionals and the board, stay focused, set the right pace, recruit allies, build momentum, engage skeptics, pick our battles, calm the waters, change the culture, follow our conscience, and press on. All the while, we have to weather a barrage of criticism, treat others with respect (even if they don't return the favor), and try to repair strained relationships. This requires deep reservoirs of optimism, determination, courage, and stamina, making "persevere" the hardest of the "Six Ps" in this book.

Remember:

- Nonprofits cannot move in a new direction unless a critical mass of professionals, volunteers, and funders support it.

- To nurture this support, nonprofits need to stay focused, set the right pace, recruit allies, and use each success to build momentum for the next step.
- Since there is almost always resistance, a nonprofit needs to invest time and effort in getting dissenters on board or, if they can't be moved, in preserving ties with them.
- While a nonprofit needs to pick its battles, on major issues, principle—not politics—should be its guide.

CHAPTER 6

PRIORITIZE

Set Priorities with "The Three Questions"

EARLY IN MY TIME as dean, a graduate offered to donate a yacht to Columbia Law School. I was excited until I heard the condition he set for the gift: to maximize his tax deduction, we could not sell the yacht for several years. Instead, we had to use it in our teaching or research. "Why don't you have your faculty teach seminars on it?" he suggested. Needless to say, I appreciated his commitment to the school and would have liked to add this gift to our fundraising totals. But I saw no value in a floating law school classroom—which, to be honest, sounds a bit like the premise of a sitcom. We passed on the gift.

A law school—and, indeed, every well-run nonprofit—has to stay focused on its mission. But even then, there is always too much to do. Nonprofits have to be selective, since "nobody is ever overrun with great prosperity," joked Bishop Michael Saporito of the Archdiocese of Newark.

Yet unlike "Con-Law cruises," many of the ideas we can't pursue are very appealing. Which promising initiatives do we have to shelve? What needs should not be addressed? These are poignant and difficult questions.

We need to answer them wisely, or we will end up wasting scarce resources. As management guru Peter Drucker observed in his book, *People and Performance*, well-run institutions don't just "do things right." They also "do the right things."

So setting priorities is critical at nonprofits, but it also is especially difficult. Unlike for-profit firms, they cannot use profitability to compare alternatives. Rather, nonprofits have to figure out which programs maximize *social* return—that is, which advance the mission most effectively. Yet this is easier said than done. How can nonprofits operationalize this abstract goal?

This chapter recommends the decision-making criteria we developed at JDC, introduced in chapter 4, which I call "the three questions":

- How important is the problem we are trying to solve?
- How effective is our response?
- Are we the right organization to respond?

In my experience, these questions are an exceedingly effective way to set priorities. The questions are jargon-free and should be intuitive for professionals and board members with very different skill sets. In other words, they are easy to use. Although the questions are broad enough to apply to any nonprofit, they can be tailored to the specifics of each organization's work.

As chapter 5 emphasized, even the best ideas fail unless there is buy-in for them. How should a nonprofit "sell" the three questions to its professionals and board? Just as JDC used an inclusive process to develop them, as chapter 4 explained, other nonprofits should take a similar approach. The three questions should be a starting point, and key stakeholders should be asked to tailor them to their organization's unique mission, goals, and culture.

DON'T JUST FOLLOW THE MONEY

Before exploring how nonprofits *should* set priorities, it is important to clarify how they should *not* do it. Nonprofits should not simply "follow the money," running programs that are popular with donors but do not advance the mission most effectively.

"You can't lose sight of donor interests," observed Eric Goldstein of UJA. "But you can't take a big multi-million dollar gift from a donor that distracts you from your mission."

Nonprofits should be careful about "coming up with some glitzy new thing" just to please a donor, cautions Leonard Leo of The Federalist Society, whose mission is to promote a conservative vision of the law. "It's going to draw energy and focus away from other things that are really important."

Instead, nonprofit professionals should ask for gifts that advance the mission most effectively. The planning process should produce a menu of options, as chapter 4 explained.

Donors still are free to suggest ideas that are not on a nonprofit's wish list. If their idea is compelling—so it deserves to be on the list—a nonprofit should take the gift. A nonprofit's professionals do not have a monopoly on good ideas, and donors can add value in offering a fresh perspective.

Yet if professionals are skeptical about a donor's suggestion, they should not accept funding for it. If their assessment is correct, the idea is not the best use of scarce resources. Even if they are mistaken, the initiative won't succeed unless they believe in it. Subpar work tarnishes a nonprofit's reputation and undermines morale.

In addition, donors rarely cover an initiative's full cost. Even if they fund the direct costs, they might not pay for the office space, utility bills, oversight by senior managers, and other indirect costs. So although we may be tempted to say, "what the heck, it's free," it probably isn't. Instead, "if we take too many of these gifts, we'll go broke," as my friend Nick Lemann once joked when he was dean of Columbia Journalism School.

Admittedly, it isn't easy to say "no" to gifts. At a nonprofit, we are conditioned to chase after them, not turn them down. It's good for the nonprofit's reputation (and our own) to bring in more money. Extra funding also means more programs, employees, and other good things. So for many people—myself included—passing on a gift is like turning down our favorite dessert. It takes willpower, but sometimes it has to be done.

THE FIRST QUESTION: HOW IMPORTANT IS THE PROBLEM WE ARE TRYING TO SOLVE?

In setting priorities, if we shouldn't just "follow the money," what should we do instead? What should we prioritize? To figure this out, I recommend using "the three questions."

These questions are rooted in a fundamental insight: the social value of a nonprofit's work depends on both the importance of its goals and its effectiveness in achieving them. The first of the three questions focuses on goals, while the second considers effectiveness. Specifically, the first question asks, "How important is the problem we are trying to solve?"

Potential Payoff

To answer this question, we need to consider the potential payoff. What happens if the nonprofit achieves its goal? "How many people benefit," William MacAskill explains in *Doing Good Better*, "and by how much?" Doing more good per dollar is the key to effective altruism, an idea he has championed.

The potential impact varies with the nonprofit's mission. An advocacy organization can highlight the importance of its cause, while a religious organization can emphasize the value of moral guidance, community, good works, and spiritual fulfillment. A university can invoke the professional advantages of higher education for students as well as the value of research.

Shifting Needs

The benefits from accomplishing a particular goal evolve over time. In investigating these changes, the first question weeds out missions that have become stale. If a nonprofit was formed to address a problem that has now been solved, the first question presses the nonprofit to shut down or find a new mission.

This question highlights not just whether things have gotten better but also whether they have gotten worse. Sometimes a task that used to be easy suddenly becomes infinitely harder.

Columbia Law School faced this sort of jarring shift during the financial crisis of 2008. All of a sudden, our students were struggling to find jobs. This was a 180-degree change. In ordinary times, our students were in high demand. When I would visit law firms, it felt like the senior partners wanted to rummage through my pockets, looking for the names of promising students to recruit.

But everything changed in the fall of 2008, when a severe economic downturn slashed the demand for legal services. In response, most leading law firms cut their entering classes in half. One reduced the number from eighty to twelve, and a few decided not to hire anyone. In other words, Columbia Law School's answer to the first question—how important is the problem?—had changed dramatically for job placement.

The idea that students with us during the "Great Recession" would not find jobs was simply unacceptable. These students were every bit as good as those who came before them, and they deserved the same professional opportunities. So we mobilized to address this unexpected challenge.

To supplement the tireless efforts of our career counseling team, I became the school's "headhunter-in-chief." Every week, the team provided an updated list of students who were still looking for jobs. When one of these students had an interview, I personally called people they met, as did colleagues on the faculty. This was a new level of effort for us.

Since there were not enough jobs at law firms, we looked for other opportunities. For example, we reached out to the general counsels of corporations, who regularly hired our graduates—but only after they had worked at a law firm for a few years. Why not hire them straight from law school instead?

To make this case, I called Brad Smith, a Columbia graduate who was general counsel of Microsoft (and later became the company's vice chair and president). "If you hire our alums when they graduate, they will be very loyal to Microsoft," I said, "and the starting salary doesn't have to be lavish." I then suggested a number. Brad thought for a few seconds before answering. "I like your idea, so I am going to create four entry-level positions," he said. "But if it's okay with you, I'm going to pay them twice what you suggested."

With Brad's permission, I called more than one hundred other general counsels over the next few weeks, describing his plan and urging them to do the same. Unfortunately, many of these general counsels were in no position to hire anyone—indeed, some told me they themselves were being laid off. But a number decided to create new entry-level positions.

These new opportunities, our calls to law firms, and a range of other initiatives got us where we needed to be. In ordinary times, between 95 percent and 99 percent of our graduates are placed in jobs immediately after graduation. In these difficult years, we were able to stay within this range. But it took more effort than ever before. Fortunately, things went back to normal after a few years. But for about half of my years as dean, job placement was front and center—something I never would have predicted when I started. The first question—how important is the problem we are trying to solve?—focuses attention on this sort of rapid change in needs.

Daunting Comparisons

The first question also presses nonprofits to make comparisons. Among the various goals they can pursue, which has the potential to add the most value?

These comparisons are especially difficult when goals are very different. Is it more important to shelter the homeless or clean a polluted river? Again, unlike for-profit firms, which can use profits to compare the value of alternatives, nonprofits don't have this sort of uniform metric.

Even so, nonprofits can still show that their goal is important, even if they cannot show that it is *more important* than other (very different) goals. In making this case, they should not rely on intuition or anecdotes. "One person's success story does not mean the program caused that success," Mary Kay Gugerty and Dean Karlan have observed in their book, *The Goldilocks Challenge*. "And one person's success story does not mean that everyone in the program succeeded or even, on average, the program succeeded." Instead, nonprofits should make the case with analysis and data.

Although comparing *very different* missions or goals is daunting, comparing *similar* ones is much easier. For example, once a nonprofit decides to provide social services to needy people, data and analysis can clarify which populations are neediest.

This comparison is essential at JDC, whose mission is to help needy Jews and other vulnerable populations in seventy countries around the world. The first question presses JDC to determine which are most vulnerable.

In our "Global Strategy for Programs," which we posted online every year while I was CEO, we included a detailed chart with the GDP per capita in different countries where JDC works. For example, in 2019, compared to $64,768 in the United States, the number was $42,144 in Israel, $12,507 in Poland, $6,477 in Belarus, and $3,221 in Ukraine. The same chart also showed how much JDC was spending in different places. Not surprisingly, we generally focused on places with lower GDP per capita. In deciding which clients to prioritize, we also looked at their other sources of support, including government benefits, other nonprofits, and their families.

During my time as CEO, the data showed that our neediest clients were elderly Jews in the former Soviet Union (like Olga, who is mentioned in chapter 1). Many of these clients live in Ukraine, the poorest country in Europe. Ukraine and other post-Soviet countries have a weaker social safety net for the elderly than most other countries. The state pension in Ukraine was only two dollars per day in 2019. To live on this amount, someone often has to choose between buying food or medicine. By comparison, the daily pension in 2019 was 7.5 times larger in Hungary (fifteen dollars), sixteen times larger in France (thirty-two dollars), and twenty-five times larger in the United States (fifty dollars).

Elderly Jews in the former Soviet Union are especially needy for two other reasons as well. First, they have very little savings because they lived most of their professional lives under Communism. Second, many are all alone. Their relatives were among the 1.5 million Jews who left for Israel, Germany, and the United States over the past three decades. Unlike seniors who live with their children—a common practice in the former Soviet Union—elderly Jews often have no one to care for them.

So in answering the first question, JDC concluded that addressing the abject poverty of these clients was our most important challenge. In response, we committed $145 million in 2020, which was almost 40 percent of JDC's $371 million of spending in 2020.

To sum up, the first question considers the importance of the problems a nonprofit seeks to solve. Is the mission still relevant or has it become stale? What new problems are on the horizon? Using data and analysis, a nonprofit should demonstrate the social value of achieving its goals. If it succeeds, would it reach a significant number of people? Would it make a meaningful difference in their lives?

THE SECOND QUESTION: HOW EFFECTIVE IS OUR RESPONSE?

Choosing the right goal is critically important, but it's not enough. Nonprofits must pursue it the right way. Otherwise, they are wasting time and money. So in setting priorities, nonprofits need to make sure they can "move the needle" on the issues they target. This is why the second question is, "How effective is the nonprofit's response?"

Impact and Cost-Effectiveness

In answering this question, nonprofits should focus on two issues: impact and cost. To show impact, a nonprofit needs to deliver both quantity and quality. For example, if the mission is to feed hungry people, how many people are being served? Are they the neediest clients? Is the food nutritious and appealing?

The key issue is not impact alone but impact *per dollar*. A nonprofit should spend as little as possible to achieve its goals. Admittedly, focusing on costs can feel coldhearted. At some point, we all want to say, "How can we count pennies while people are suffering?" But if we waste money, we can't do as much good. To provide better service to more people, we need to be efficient—indeed, ruthlessly so.

At JDC, it is a source of pride that the organization can change lives with very modest investments. To show this impressive social return, the annual plan we posted on the website included a table with the average amount we spent per client in various programs. For example, food and medicine for an elderly client in the former Soviet Union cost only $283 per year in 2019, while home care cost only $1,180 per year. (The number is higher for Holocaust survivors, since the German government funds additional services for them.) This extraordinary impact per dollar isn't possible in the United States, where costs are much higher.

Measuring Impact: Outputs, Outcomes, and Indirect Measures

This brings us to an important question: how should nonprofits measure their impact? The most basic metric, which I just used, is the quantity of goods and services a nonprofit produces, which are called "outputs." How much of each type of good or service does a nonprofit provide? How many beneficiaries does it serve? On average, how much does it spend per beneficiary? Do these costs vary a lot? What causes these variations? Nonprofits need this kind of information to target the right beneficiaries, cut costs, and fine-tune the mix of goods and services they offer.

Although outputs convey useful information, they don't always tell us whether a program actually works. For example, if the goal is to train unemployed coal miners to work in other industries, we don't just want to know how many people enroll. The real question is whether they get jobs. This sort of direct measure of progress is called an "outcome." While they are more illuminating than outputs, outcomes also are usually harder to track.

Sometimes nonprofits try to measure them indirectly. For example, reputation surveys convey whether third parties *believe* a nonprofit is effective. Yet a survey is reliable only if participants are well-informed and objective and the right questions are asked.

Because outcomes can be hard to measure, a nonprofit sometimes can avoid this challenge by simply tracking outputs, as long as they are a reasonable proxy for social return. For example, if desperately poor clients would die without food and medicine—as is the case with JDC's clients in the former Soviet Union—outputs such as the quantity of food and medicine delivered, the number of clients who receive them, and the average cost of supplying these items give a meaningful sense of social return.

Sometimes this causal link between outputs and outcomes is not obvious initially, but the right research can establish it. Sarah Hemminger had plenty of data to show that the nonprofit she founded was extremely effective. In matching students with supportive volunteers, Thread accepts only young people performing in the bottom 25 percent of their class—a group that historically has had a very low high school graduation rate. "If you look at freshmen in Baltimore City High Schools with GPAs less than 1.0," Sarah explained, "historically only 6 percent graduate from high school in four years." By contrast, when students with these GPAs enroll in Thread, 65 percent graduate in four years—a rate that is more than ten times better than their peers.

Yet although this data is powerful evidence that the program works, it doesn't show *how* it works, so it doesn't reveal ways to make Thread *even more* effective. "You need to be able to performance-manage to one metric," Sarah explained, "like a corporation with dollars." As a trained biomedical engineer, Sarah was well equipped to find the answer. "We went back and looked at all the data because luckily we collect a lot, and we found that the answer is touch points," she explained. "The number of interactions between a young person and a volunteer in a given month is predictive of things like high school graduation."

Once they established this causal link between touch points (an output) and graduation (an outcome), Sarah and her team started monitoring the touch points of each Thread student. "That led us to build a mobile app that allows us to track touch points in real time," she explained, "so I can see red, yellow, green, where there are breaks in the relational capacity in the community."

One Size Does Not Fit All

Most nonprofits don't have a CEO who is a biomedical engineer. But with creativity and persistence, every nonprofit can find ways to measure its progress. The right metric varies with a nonprofit's work. Hospitals should track health outcomes and error rates, while advocacy organizations should track litigation "win rates," the favorable precedents they set, and the like.

As a law school dean, I was an information junkie. I was especially interested in our student-faculty ratio, since a lower ratio allows a school to nurture closer ties between students and faculty, field a broader and more innovative curriculum, and cover more areas of expertise in research.

To pay for a larger faculty, we had to raise more money. We used data to track our fundraising progress, identify opportunities, and revise our approach; on average, we raised more than twice what the school used to raise before I became dean.

We also scrutinized job placements as well as the ever-improving credentials of our entering classes. We pored over student course evaluations, and we asked faculty members for detailed annual reports on their research, teaching, service, media appearances, and other work. In combination, these various sources provided a clear picture of how we were doing.

Admittedly, some missions are harder to quantify. The value of a house of worship turns in part on faith, which cannot be measured or even verified. Can you picture a PowerPoint slide on "afterlife placement rates"? Yet these institutions still provide some goods and services that are straightforward to evaluate. It is easy to track the size of their membership, attendance at religious services, the frequency and popularity of other programming, and member satisfaction.

It is hard to think of something more ineffable than spiritual development. Yet the Institute for Priestly Formation, which seeks to enhance this quality in seminarians and parish priests, found a creative way to measure progress. The Institute asks participants to fill out the same survey before and after the program. Participants use a scale of 1 ("never") to 7 ("always") to offer observations about themselves. On average, they register increases of more than one point on a range of questions, such as "I am experiencing and understanding how to integrate the gift of spiritual discernment with my pastoral service."

Similarly, the mission of museums, orchestras, and other cultural organizations—beauty, meaning, and inspiration—also are hard to quantify, but an indirect measure is easy to track: the size of the audience. These organizations also get feedback from expert critics.

There are risks in relying on imperfect proxies for social return. Nonprofits might overemphasize features they are measuring, while neglecting key goals their metrics don't track. As the old adage says, "What gets measured gets done." For example, if schools are evaluated by graduation rates alone—with no effort to ensure that graduates have the necessary skills—there is a temptation to award diplomas to unqualified students. Even so, the right response to this challenge is to fine-tune the metric, not to abandon efforts to monitor progress.

Easier Comparisons

In answering the second question, nonprofits should ask not only whether a specific response is effective but whether other responses might be *more* effective. This inquiry, which is called "cost-effectiveness" analysis, seeks the most efficient way to accomplish a goal. Fortunately, comparing different ways to pursue the *same* goal is easier than comparing *different* goals.

For example, although there is no uniform metric to tell us whether to house the homeless or clean a polluted river, our job gets easier once we decide to clean the river. With data and analysis, we can decide whether to use filters, microorganisms that consume the pollution, incentives for polluters to change their ways, or another alternative.

Usually, the right approach is to run pilot programs, which test different alternatives. Like high-tech start-ups, nonprofits should "experiment and fail and learn from that failure and improve," observed Asha Curran, CEO of GivingTuesday, "because that's the path to ultimate success."

"I think you take a bit of a portfolio approach," observed Peter Lehner of Natural Resources Defense Council (NRDC) and Earthjustice. Along with implementing initiatives "where you are pretty sure you'll be able to make a difference," nonprofits should also try riskier strategies. "Ideally, they have some synergies amongst each other."

Impact Multipliers

To maximize their impact per dollar, nonprofits should favor programs with particular features, which I call "impact multipliers." These features are likely to offer extra "bang for the buck."

An Ounce of Prevention

Since "an ounce of prevention is worth a pound of cure," heading off a problem usually is more efficient than picking up the pieces later. Any nonprofit can multiply its impact in this way. For example, preventing pollution is often cheaper than cleaning it up. Likewise, social service organizations usually get better results by intervening early in their clients' lives. Keeping children on track often is more effective than helping adults turn their lives around.

Teach Them to Fish

Nonprofits can maximize impact not only by heading off a problem but also by empowering people to address it themselves. As the old saying goes, "give a man a fish and you feed him for a day; *teach* a man to fish and you feed him for a lifetime."

Job training can be transformative not only for the clients themselves but also for their families. "Going from a $25,000 job to a $38,000 job can be the difference between crisis and stability," noted Eric Goldstein of UJA. Likewise, nonprofits can also multiply impact by treating substance abuse, offering child care so single mothers can work, empowering people with disabilities to live on their own and, of course, providing higher education.

Help the Helpers

A nonprofit can multiply its impact by empowering individuals to change not only their own lives but also the lives of others. If someone wants to aid vulnerable populations, strengthen communities, or address other urgent social needs, why not help them do it? This can be a very cost-effective way to advance a cause.

For example, when graduates work in government or nonprofits, Columbia Law School helps pay off their student loans. This funding makes it financially feasible for more graduates to do this socially valuable work. As dean, I was proud to make Columbia's program the most generous in the nation—a distinction we held for about two weeks, until Yale announced a (slightly) more generous program.

Along with empowering individuals, a nonprofit also can "help the helpers" by assisting other organizations. This is a core strategy of JFNA, an umbrella organization representing local Jewish federations. For example, during the COVID-19 pandemic, JFNA helped other nonprofits claim urgently needed federal aid so they could continue their important work. The Small Business Administration (SBA) was offering forgivable loans to cover employees' salaries, but the application process was daunting. "We knew that the nonprofit sector did not have experience applying for SBA loans," recalled CEO Eric Fingerhut. In response, JFNA offered webinars, a hotline, and other training. "We took something that was complicated," Eric said. "We made it simple. We repeated it over and over again." With this surgical (and rapid) investment of time and effort, JFNA helped other nonprofits tap hundreds of millions of dollars in emergency relief.

Similarly, the Robin Hood Foundation has "helped the helpers" by urging the New York City government to pay more promptly when it hires nonprofit social service providers. "We had organizations that were taking out loans, making employment decisions, and making programmatic decisions based on the fact that they have this massive amount of receivables coming in" from the city, observed former CEO Wes Moore. "There is no grant that is going to make up for that." So instead, Robin Hood engaged in advocacy, using "every lever that Robin Hood has, whether it's influential people on our board, whether it's our policy expertise and data, whether it's the fact that we fund more than

500 organizations in the city," he continued. "Our leverage is pretty significant."

Influence the Influencers

Along with helping the helpers, nonprofits also can multiply their impact by influencing the influencers. When the goal is to alter public attitudes, a nonprofit can amplify its impact by changing the views of influential people, who then help spread the word.

For example, in seeking to advance disability rights, the Ruderman Family Foundation has targeted Hollywood. "We firmly believe entertainment shapes public attitudes, and I think we've gone a long way toward injecting authentic portrayals of disability into popular entertainment," explained Jay Ruderman, the foundation's president. "I think that will have a ripple effect on how people around the world see people with disabilities," leading to "more employment of people with disabilities, more acceptance in the community."

To highlight the underrepresentation of actors with disabilities, Jay faulted Alec Baldwin for playing a blind character in the 2016 movie *Blind*. "We got a lot of press," Jay said, "because the thing that the news likes to write about the most is celebrity." The foundation followed up with research, documenting that 95 percent of characters with disabilities are played by able-bodied actors, and that a high percentage of the Oscars for best actor in recent years went to able-bodied actors playing characters with disabilities.

In response, Hollywood institutions began working with the foundation. "Our biggest success in the industry," Jay observed, "has been to get ViacomCBS, Sony Pictures Studios, NBCUniversal, and Paramount Pictures to agree to open their auditions to all actors with disabilities." The foundation also awards the Ruderman Seal of Approval for Authentic Representation to TV shows and movies that offer substantial speaking roles to performers with disabilities. To help build a pipeline of actors with disabilities, the foundation funded a scholarship at the David Geffen School of Drama at Yale University and the Academy of Motion

Pictures Arts and Sciences' Gold Rising Program. The foundation also works with other key institutions, such as the Sundance Film Festival and the Academy Awards. "At the [2020] Oscars ceremony, you had an actor with a disability presenting an award," added Shira Ruderman, the Foundation's executive director. "This never happened before."

Admittedly, not every nonprofit will be able to influence the Academy Awards, but all organizations should be strategic in spreading the word about their cause. By winning over athletes, actors, politicians, or other prominent people, a nonprofit can speak through their voices, reaching a wider audience.

Bring Others Along

A nonprofit also can multiply its impact by recruiting partners who supply additional expertise or resources. Finding the right partners is a key priority for Rachel Garbow Monroe, the president and CEO of the Harry and Jeanette Weinberg Foundation, which allocates approximately $150 million of annual grants to provide direct services to vulnerable populations.

In launching an initiative to transform the libraries in Baltimore City Public Schools, Rachel and her colleagues prioritized this project not only because the need was urgent but also because others would help. Federal, state, and local governments and other public sources funded the renovation of building facilities but did not have the flexibility to cover books, computer terminals, e-readers, furniture, or staffing, so the foundation stepped in to fill this gap. The Foundation also recruited almost forty other nonprofit and corporate partners, who launched summer literacy programs, food bank programs, outreach to parents, and much more.

The results are impressive. Book checkouts in these libraries rose 400 percent in four years, and reading fluency scores in these schools rose dramatically, outperforming other schools. "We couldn't do this alone," Rachel emphasized.

Share Good Ideas

Nonprofits can persuade others not just to join them, but also to replace them. When nonprofits come up with a good idea, they can multiply their impact by convincing others to adopt it.

Admittedly, this is not the way for-profit firms do business. They usually want to protect their trade secrets and market share. But a nonprofit's priority should be its mission, not its competitive position.

Who should borrow a good idea? The government is an especially promising candidate, since it has the capacity to scale it up. This is what happened when United Way of Metropolitan Dallas launched an initiative called "Destination Graduation" at a local public high school, which provided mentors, standardized test prep, and resources for educating parents. "We went in and developed a program that became replicable" and was introduced to other schools, explained CEO Jennifer Sampson, "until we realized, 'You know what? This is a program the school district should lead.'" Since the program was generating strong results, the school district agreed. "Ultimately they put the program resource requirements in their own budgets and United Way sunset out of it," she continued, "but we did a lot of great work on the front end to get that flywheel going."

As United Way's experience highlights, nonprofits have a comparative advantage as incubators, facing fewer political and bureaucratic constraints in launching and testing new ideas. Yet the government has an edge as an operator because it has more resources and benefits from economies of scale.

While the transfer of promising ideas to the government usually is informal and unplanned, JDC has pioneered a more systematic approach in Israel. JDC partners with government ministries to test new ways to deliver social services. For each dollar JDC invests in these pilot programs, the government invests almost two dollars (on average). Instead of running the day-to-day operations itself, JDC recruits other nonprofits to play this role, so more organizations learn the new approach and help perfect it. If the new idea succeeds, the government takes over the program, covers the full cost, and implements it throughout the country. The other nonprofits facilitate this transition and often remain involved, while JDC exits the project, so it can move on to test other promising ideas.

In this division of labor, JDC functions like a venture capitalist for social services, constantly incubating innovations. This approach offers a compelling answer to the second question, "how effective is a nonprofit's response?" With an investment that is temporary and relatively modest, JDC can transform the way social services are delivered throughout the country.

Red Flags

Along with identifying favorable features, the second question also helps uncover problems. Are nonprofits using a dated approach? Or targeting the wrong beneficiaries? Or spending more than necessary? If the answer is "yes," nonprofits should respond to these red flags by either fixing or ending the flawed program.

Mission Accomplished

One reason to change course is that a nonprofit has accomplished its goal. For example, the March of Dimes initially was launched to cure polio. Once a vaccine was found, the organization needed a new mission. It now focuses more broadly on the health of mothers and babies.

Often this new goal builds on prior successes. For example, JDC has worked for decades to revive Jewish communal life in Central and Eastern Europe, which was devastated by the Holocaust and decades of Communist rule.

An early goal was to build a cohort of local leaders. To recruit them, it made sense to defer to them in deciding what JDC would support. This was an effective way to "bring them to the table."

Fortunately, this goal had largely been accomplished by the time I became CEO: there already was an impressive group of local leaders. As the next step, we wanted to work with these leaders on shared goals, such as enhancing their communities' capacity to care for vulnerable people. In this effort, there was still value in deferring to local leaders, if only to secure their buy-in. But we could do this by offering a more bounded choice. Instead of saying, "We'll work with you on anything," the message was, "We'd like to work with you on any of the options on this list, so let's talk about what might interest you." (How did we figure out which options to offer? The three questions, of course!)

Declining Demand

Nonprofits should take a hard look at a program not only when its goal has been achieved, but also when demand for it declines. One reason this can happen is competition. For example, if a hospital is losing patients to a crosstown rival, its leaders need to figure out why. Is it charging too much? Or is quality the issue? Or customer service? To attract more patients, the hospital needs to raise its game.

Demand also can decline when the need becomes less acute. For example, if a neighborhood becomes more commercial and less residential, the demand for youth and family programming there is likely to diminish.

Unnecessary Expenses

Even if demand remains robust, another red flag is bloated costs. In answering the second question, nonprofits should calculate their unit cost. How much do they spend on each beneficiary? In calculating this figure, nonprofits should consider *all* relevant expenses, including overhead and other fixed costs. Are there ways to cut any of these costs?

Every little bit counts. As a law school dean, I worked with a terrific CFO, Ed Moroni, who spent decades at Columbia and knew it inside out. In one of our first meetings, he said something that has always stuck with me. "Saving $10,000 may not seem like much in a $100 million budget," he said, "but if you can do it every week, that's more than half a million dollars a year." By constantly finding modest savings, every nonprofit can cut its budget by a meaningful amount over the course of the year.

To sum up, in asking whether a nonprofit's response is effective, the second question presses organizations to maximize their impact and find cheaper ways to get the job done. To offer a compelling answer to this question, nonprofits need to track progress, compare alternatives, and test improvements. They should look for impact multipliers and avoid red flags. In short, they need to deliver results.

THE THIRD QUESTION: ARE WE THE RIGHT ORGANIZATION TO RESPOND?

In deciding whether to prioritize an initiative, a nonprofit is off to a strong start if it has persuasive answers to the first two questions: "How important is the problem?" and "How effective is our response?" But this is not enough. The nonprofit should also ask a third question that, in my experience, is not asked often enough: "Are *we* the right organization to respond?"

To answer this question, a nonprofit needs to consider what other organizations are doing, focusing on two issues. First, how much attention are others paying to the issue? "We can make a much bigger difference," effective altruism proponent William MacAskill has emphasized in his book, *Doing Good Better*, "if we focus our efforts on areas on which comparatively fewer resources have been spent." In other words, a nonprofit can add more value by focusing on issues that others have neglected.

Second, does the organization have a comparative advantage in addressing the issue? Nonprofits add more value by playing to their strengths. "You can't be all things to all people," cautioned Bishop Michael Saporito of the Archdiocese of Newark, "so you have to figure out, 'What is our big thing?'"

"We have a very simple rule internally," observed Leonard Leo of The Federalist Society. "An organization can only do one or two things really well. Once you start stretching beyond that, you're probably not going to be particularly effective."

If others have an edge, the wisest course usually is to leave the job to them. "If I find out that you're doing this better, why should I still do it?" observed Carol Baldwin Moody of Legal Momentum. "If I can contribute something, I'll stay in it. But if not, I've got a very small staff."

The Only Game in Town

When a nonprofit is the only one addressing an issue, its answer to the third question is compelling. "I like to be in areas which are not crowded," Jay Ruderman observed about his family's foundation. "We really look for a vacuum, an area that isn't well funded. If not a lot of attention is paid to it, we go narrow and deep." Yet when others start focusing on the issue, Jay's analysis changes. "Once we're involved in a field that then becomes populated, and there are many different actors," he continued, "that's my cue that I can exit and do something else."

Her Justice also looks for gaps to fill. In providing volunteer lawyers to women living in poverty, the organization focuses on cases that others do not take. For instance, "it's very hard to get free representation on child support cases," explained Amy Barasch, the executive director. Unfortunately, fathers sometimes hide income as a way to reduce the support they are required to pay. In those cases, "it's actually really hard for an unrepresented person to make that case to the court," Amy explained, "so those are the cases we take." On average, Her Justice's clients receive a 70 percent increase in child support. "That could be the difference," Amy continued, "between whether or not they can really raise their kids in New York City."

Museums also look for a unique niche. When Ellen Futter became president of the American Museum of Natural History, one of her first initiatives was to renovate the Planetarium. A key reason was that it was a "strategic differentiator," as she put it. "The planetarium was wildly out of date and something had to be done," she explained. "We also saw it as a unique vehicle for making a statement about modernity." When

Ellen began her service as president, "there was a perception that the museum was a little musty and dusty," she observed, "and we wanted to show that this was no longer going to be the case." The Planetarium's distinctive architecture—a sphere in a glass box—"was hugely symbolic of an institution that was moving into a modern era in a modern way."

Social service organizations also look for unique ways to add value. For example, JDC prioritizes elderly Jews in the former Soviet Union not only because they are so needy but also because they have nowhere else to turn. Government safety nets in the region are very limited, and local Jewish communities do not yet have the capacity to supplement them. Instead, these frail clients depend on JDC and the organizations that partner with it in this work, including the Claims Conference, Jewish federations, the International Fellowship of Christians and Jews, World Jewish Relief, the Wohl Legacy, and others. Yet aside from JDC and its partners, other international NGOs generally were not caring for these elderly clients when I was CEO.

Comparative Advantage

Of course, a nonprofit is rarely the only game in town. When a problem is important, other organizations usually also try to address it. "The chances of you doing what you're doing and being the first," observed Wes Moore, governor of Maryland and former CEO of Robin Hood, "it's hard, because most things in this world have been tried before."

When others do similar work, nonprofits should push themselves—frankly, more than they usually do—to justify why they also should do it. The third question presses them to prioritize work that others cannot do as effectively. What are the nonprofit's unique strengths?

In his classic management text, *Good to Great*, Jim Collins offers similar advice to for-profit firms: figure out "what you can be the best in the world at (and, equally important, what you cannot be the best in the world at)."

When a nonprofit does not have a comparative advantage in addressing an issue, it should leave the job to others who do. "Our objectives are very clear in terms of what we were going to do," observed Leonard Leo of the Federalist Society. "Where we were presented with opportunities that really didn't fit directly within that, we took a pass."

Similarly, at United Way of Metropolitan Dallas, "our strategy is tightly defined and we are very clear about our priorities," explained CEO Jennifer Sampson. "We can be wildly creative within that space, but guardrails are in place to prevent us from moving outside of the strategy."

Expertise

Sometimes a nonprofit's comparative advantage is its expertise. For example, some hospitals treat cancer, while others deliver babies. Some environmental organizations bring lawsuits, while others make their case in the political arena, and still others do research. Even though their missions are similar, their core competencies are very different. Before taking on an issue, a nonprofit should make sure it has the right expertise. If it doesn't (and others do), it is probably not right for the job.

Location

Along with expertise, a nonprofit's location also can provide a comparative advantage. For example, a law school based in Washington, DC can offer students more opportunities to volunteer in federal agencies during the academic year.

Likewise, Columbia Law School's location in New York City is a key advantage for research and teaching about industries concentrated there, including finance, the media, publishing, theater, the arts, high tech, and real estate. Columbia also benefits from proximity to leading law firms, the United Nations, and the host of public interest organizations based in New York.

New York is so alluring that other schools sometimes try to capitalize on its mystique. Before Elena Kagan became a Supreme Court justice, she was a very successful dean of Harvard Law School. A native New Yorker herself, she sometimes referred to Harvard as "the New York

City of law schools," presumably in an effort to convey the breadth and depth of Harvard's curriculum. A group of prospective students who were visiting Columbia after a trip to Harvard once repeated this phrase and asked me to comment. "Harvard is very appealing," I said with a smile, "but I'm pretty sure it's in Massachusetts."

Synergies

Nonprofits develop comparative advantages not only when they have the right location and expertise but also when one aspect of their mission makes them more effective at another. These synergies arise in various ways.

One is through easier access. When services are bundled together, beneficiaries can find them in a single institution. For example, UJA has launched one-stop social service hubs with food pantries, legal services, job training, counseling, and other services for people facing hard times. "You might come in because of the food," explained Eric Goldstein of UJA, "but while you are there, you can access other services that can change the cycle" of poverty.

Delivering services together also can enhance quality. For example, two of Legal Momentum's initiatives to advance the rights of women—impact litigation and a helpline—reinforce each other. To establish a new precedent, Legal Momentum looks for the right case. The issue should affect many women and the facts should be sympathetic. These cases often come from the helpline. While its main purpose is to answer questions and refer clients to other service providers, the helpline "often gives us the case that will have impact if we bring it," CEO Carol Baldwin Moody observed.

This sort of synergy is common at other nonprofits as well. For example, most houses of worship offer community service and educational activities along with religious services. "Preaching is not just what you want people to know," emphasized Bishop Michael Saporito, "but what you want them to do."

To be clear, these are all examples of synergies because an important condition is satisfied: all the activities are closely connected to the mission. But what if one of them isn't? What if an emergency room starts offering music lessons to children? In that case, we don't have a synergy; we have mission creep.

Even if both initiatives are core to the mission, running them together does not always enhance quality; sometimes the opposite is true. For example, a humanitarian organization, which delivers social services around the world, usually should shy away from political advocacy. If the organization antagonizes local authorities by protesting their policies, it faces greater obstacles in providing care. To avoid this negative synergy, it has to leave advocacy to other organizations.

Differentiating Your Work

In urging nonprofits to identify their comparative advantages, the third question presses organizations to prioritize work that is not only important and effective but also unique. They add more value in doing things that others can't or won't do.

JDC took this lesson to heart in crafting its strategy to strengthen Jewish communities in the former Soviet Union. This work yields compelling answers to the first two questions. It clearly is important, and JDC's efforts have been quite effective. Yet the third question is more challenging, since other organizations are also engaged in this effort. (During my time as CEO, JDC and its partners were the only game in town in elder care, but not in community development.) So what can JDC do that is unique and leverages JDC's comparative advantages?

As a law school dean, when I had to choose among competing options, I received wise advice from my friend Richard Richman, a successful entrepreneur with degrees from both the law and business schools at Columbia. "Define your goal very precisely," he would say. "Once you know what you are really trying to do, you can tell which option is best."

Applying this "Richman Test," what specifically is JDC trying to accomplish in reviving Jewish communities in post-Soviet republics? JDC actually has a different goal than other nonprofits, which is grounded in the organization's mission to care for vulnerable populations (and has obvious synergies with this effort). Even as JDC provides this care *today*, it strives to prepare local communities to bear more of this burden *in the future*. In other words, JDC seeks to build local capacity to provide care.

In contrast, other organizations have very different community development goals. At the risk of oversimplifying, the Jewish Agency for Israel promotes ties to Israel, while Chabad encourages religious observance, and World ORT focuses on education. Yet JDC's work is different. By empowering local communities to provide care, JDC adds unique value.

Avoiding Mission Creep

The third question adds value in helping nonprofits not only to figure out what they *should* do but also what they should *not* do. Avoiding distractions is critical. "You have to have a very tight and clear mission," urged Leonard Leo of The Federalist Society, "and you have to avoid mission creep."

To reinforce this point, Her Justice uses the metaphor of a fried egg. "Your core population is the yolk of the egg," Amy Barasch explained, borrowing from strategic planner Valyrie Laedlein. "That is who you exist to serve." Her Justice focuses on the yolk, while generally leaving the rest of the egg to others. For example, although Her Justice's clients often have housing problems, "that is a whole other area of really complex law," so Her Justice refers these cases to other organizations. "There are a lot of phenomenal legal services groups out there," Amy noted. "We see them as colleagues and partners, not as competition."

This discipline is important because there are powerful temptations to stray from core competencies. There is glory in addressing trendy issues, even if they are not a good fit with a nonprofit's mission and expertise. "Many groups want to be the group to bring" a high-profile challenge, cautioned Peter Lehner of Earthjustice, "so they can tell their donors that they are fighting back." Judged in part by fundraising totals, nonprofit managers are tempted to accept a gift even for an initiative they might not implement effectively. Expanded operations can be a source of prestige and even a justification for higher pay.

Yet when an initiative does not play to a nonprofit's strengths, the results are likely to be mediocre at best. Unfortunately, managers might take on the project anyway, knowing that nonprofit performance is hard to measure. If no one can tell that the work is disappointing, there is no penalty for lackluster results.

By shining a light on this risk, the third question constrains these empire-building impulses. It presses nonprofits to confirm that they can do the job well—and, ideally, better than anyone else. Otherwise, they should leave the work to others. "Learning how to say 'no' is important," explained Judith Browne Dianis of the Advancement Project. "An organization has to stay on its path and be true to who it is."

"A lot of times donors came to The Federalist Society and said, 'If you had $10 million that you didn't have today, what new bold thing would you do with it?'" Leonard Leo observed. "Our answer was pretty routinely, 'We wouldn't do anything new and bold. We would do what we're doing now. We would just scale it, because that's what we do and we know there's much more to be done there.'"

It's never easy to turn down a generous gift, but sometimes this is the best course. The third question helps us to get to the right answer. As an example, imagine that a funder approaches a humanitarian organization, offering to help it combat terrorism. Specifically, the funder offers seed funding to launch a private intelligence agency, which would identify threats and warn communities.

Is combatting terrorism part of a humanitarian organization's mission? In my view, the answer is "yes." Rescuing people from danger should be a core goal of any organization committed to helping vulnerable populations.

But is this *the right way* for a humanitarian organization to combat terrorism? Is launching an intelligence service a good match? In my opinion, the answer usually is "no." This job typically is a better fit for governments, which have surveillance powers and law enforcement agencies.

So what should the humanitarian organization say to this donor? The right answer is to turn down this gift, but that need not be the end of the conversation. Why not suggest an alternative? Ideally, there is another way to combat terrorism that draws on its comparative advantages.

For example, when I was CEO, we asked a security expert how JDC could add unique value in combatting terrorism. He offered an intriguing suggestion: "If you grow up in Israel, where terrorism is a fact of life, you learn at a young age how to identify threats," he said. "If you see an unattended backpack, you notice it and call the police. But Europeans haven't learned to look for threats when they get on a bus or walk their children to school. Someone needs to teach them."

"It's like the campaign in New York: 'If you see something, say something,'" I said. "The idea is to help people know what to look for."

"Yes, exactly. So who should teach them?" he said with a wry smile. "If only there was a one hundred-year-old organization with close ties to every Jewish community in Europe…"

"Message received," I said. It made sense to launch this initiative, since it plays to JDC's strengths.

To sum up, in asking whether a nonprofit is the right organization to respond, the third question presses nonprofits to consider what others are doing. Is the nonprofit "the only game in town"? If not—and it usually isn't—does it have something unique to add? By focusing on a nonprofit's comparative advantages, the third question prioritizes work that others cannot (or will not) do as well.

Setting the right priorities is critical. One of my most satisfying moments at JDC was a conversation with a colleague shortly before I returned to Columbia. "I assume you know this," she said, "but everyone is asking your three questions, even when you are not in the room. This has become a part of our culture, which will continue after you leave."

Remember:

- In setting priorities, nonprofits should not simply "follow the money," running programs that are popular with donors but do not advance the mission most effectively.
- Instead, nonprofits should ask "the three questions."
- **How important is the problem we are targeting?** This question focuses on the social value of a nonprofit's goals. Answering this question requires nonprofits to make difficult comparisons, as they weigh the value of addressing different problems.
- **How effective is our response?** This question presses nonprofits to be efficient in advancing their mission. Focusing on impact and cost-effectiveness, they should try to get "the most bang for the buck." Nonprofits should look for impact multipliers and shy away from red flags.
- **Are we the right organization to respond?** This question is critically important, but it's not asked often enough. The essential point is that nonprofits can add more value in doing work that others can't (or won't) do as well. As a result, nonprofits should focus on issues that others have neglected, as well as on opportunities to leverage their comparative advantages.

CHAPTER 7

PIVOT

Experiment and Innovate

WHEN THE COVID-19 PANDEMIC struck New York City, Lee Goldman had four months to go as dean of Columbia's medical school. "In your last four months of fourteen years, you expect to glide through," he recalled. "It's not very often that you face perhaps the biggest crisis of your fourteen years at the very end."

Responding quickly and forcefully, Lee urged the university to shift to online instruction. To ensure that Columbia doctors remained healthy enough to treat patients, Lee banned travel to conferences, as well as "meetings that bring together people who do the same thing," he recalled. "What if you all get sick?" Lee and his team scrambled to find protective equipment "because we couldn't ask people to take care of patients if they weren't protected." They also arranged a "massive redeployment" in which "something like 1,400 people were asked to do things they didn't usually do, anywhere from seeing patients in the emergency department to handing out protective equipment." To show support for his colleagues, Lee donned protective equipment himself to visit the emergency department and intensive care unit.

Even as Lee and his team were pivoting to meet this new challenge, they started thinking about how to pivot back once the worst of the crisis had passed. "We began early on to think about how we would ramp things back up," he recalled. They figured out how to resume medical services unrelated to the pandemic, using televisits, socially distanced in-person visits, and other innovations.

In running these creative experiments, Lee and his team modeled the fourth "P," which is "pivot": nonprofits need to search persistently— even relentlessly—for ways to improve their work. Instead of continuing on the same path, they must keep scrutinizing the "who," "what," and "how" of their work. Do they have the right team in place ("the who")? Are they pursuing the right goal ("the what")? Is there a better way to pursue it ("the how")? A nonprofit with the wrong people must replace them. Likewise, work that is outdated or subpar should be fundamentally retooled or scrapped.

Even when results are good, they can always be better. Yet this leap is challenging; success can dull a nonprofit's resolve to do better. As management guru Jim Collins famously wrote in his book, *Good to Great,* "good is the enemy of great."

To raise their game, nonprofits should improve on all fronts. How can they enhance quality? Can they do a better job of reaching the right beneficiaries? Can they help more of them? Can they get the same benefit at a lower cost? Or 90 percent of the benefit at 60 percent of the cost?

These pivots don't all have to be revolutionary. Modest ones usually are easier to dream up and less disruptive to test. "Sometimes it's really, 'let's put a little bit more salt into this batch of cookies' or 'let's try a little of this or a little of that,'" observed Sarah Hemminger, co-founder and CEO of Thread, which connects Baltimore students with volunteers. She wants colleagues to "fail forward" by testing incremental changes and learning from failures. "Where are we really?" she urges colleagues to ask. "What is the next way that we can try to improve upon that?"

"You don't have to see the whole staircase," Dr. Martin Luther King, Jr. said, "just take the first step." These incremental improvements can add up over time, turning mediocrity into excellence.

"THE WHO": BUILDING THE RIGHT TEAM

To do better work, an organization needs the right people. As Bill Gates once said, "If you took the 20 smartest people out of Microsoft, it would be an insignificant company."

Talent is as important in nonprofits as in high-tech companies. Rabbi Aviad Bodner knows this from personal experience. He left a Tel Aviv law practice representing high-tech start-ups to lead the Stanton Street Shul in lower Manhattan, nearly quadrupling the synagogue's membership in five years. "I treated the shul like it was a start-up, meaning you have very little funding, and you have a good idea," he said. "But if you don't have the right people, it's not going to work."

This view is shared by all the nonprofit leaders interviewed for this book. "Team building is everything," observed Wes Moore, governor of Maryland and former CEO of Robin Hood. "I don't care who you are, how good you are, or how smart you are. If you do not have a good set of folks around you, you will fail."

The Appeal of the Mission

A key asset in assembling the right team is the mission. Long before Kevin Washington became president and CEO of the YMCA, he forged a close personal tie to the organization. "The YMCA found me at the age of ten," he recalled. Almost every day, Kevin played basketball and other sports in afterschool programs at the YMCA in his South Philadelphia neighborhood. "That was a safe place for me," Kevin recalled. "My mother knew exactly where I was and it kept me off the streets."

After college, Kevin returned to the same YMCA in South Philadelphia to serve as its youth director. Since then, Kevin has spent more than four decades working for YMCAs across the country. He led the YMCA of Greater Hartford and the YMCA of Greater Boston before becoming the head of the national organization in 2015. Kevin is the first Black person to serve in each of these leadership roles.

"It was the place that shaped me, helping me to cross that bridge from adolescence to adulthood," Kevin recalled. "It also was the place that gave me the opportunity to do that for people in my community."

This sort of personal commitment is critical for nonprofit leaders. "As CEO of a nonprofit, you need to be doing many of the things that people assume are mother's milk at for-profit businesses, but there is a key difference," observed Eric Goldstein of UJA-Federation of NY. "For-profit CEOs move between industries because their management skills, people skills, and their ability to excel are transferable. You can have the head of an airline become the CEO of an entertainment company." But these shifts are harder in the nonprofit sector, Eric explains, because "passion for the cause is so critical."

Hiring the Right People

To harness this passion successfully, nonprofits need the right expertise, including a range of skill sets. "Get a team," observed Father Richard Gabuzda of the Institute for Priestly Formation. "Get people with different gifts." These gifts need to complement each other.

"It's a little bit like putting a basketball team together," observed Eric Fingerhut, CEO of JFNA, an umbrella organization of Jewish federations. "It's not just about finding five all-stars. It's having five all-stars that work together well, and are in the right positions."

Finding the right people can be hard, so nonprofits should be creative. For example, Ruth Raskas came to JFNA to bring private sector practices, including a focus on data. To accomplish this, she needed more colleagues with sophisticated programming skills, but they are not easy to find. "It's really hard to hire data scientists, and in some cases even traditional businesses are losing out to places like TikTok," she observed. "In the not-for-profit space you aren't paying as much" and there sometimes is less flexibility for employees to work remotely. To find the new colleagues she needed, Ruth came up with an innovative solution. "For the first time, we had a job share with Microsoft," she explained. Experts who didn't want to leave the tech sector could devote a portion of their work week to JFNA, so they could advance a cause they loved.

Who Before What

Building the right team is so important, Jim Collins argues in *Good to Great*, that leaders should focus on this first, even before they formulate their strategy to improve the organization's work. "The executives who ignited the transformations from good to great did not figure out where to drive the bus and then get people to take it there," he observed. "No, they *first* got the right people on the bus (and the wrong people off the bus) and *then* figured out where to drive it." In other words, "first who, then what."

This was my philosophy in hiring faculty. As a law school dean, I disagreed with colleagues who wanted first to decide what area of expertise we needed and then to search for candidates in that field. Rather, I wanted to hire the strongest candidates overall, regardless of the subjects they taught or areas they researched. In the language of Jim Collins, their strategy was, "first what, then who," while mine was "first who, then what."

Although this might seem like a minor disagreement—even an example of Henry Kissinger's quip that "academic politics are so vicious because the stakes are so small"—the stakes in faculty appointments are actually quite high. Tenured faculty hold appointments for life, so universities need to think carefully about these multi-decade commitments.

My reasons for focusing on "who" before "what" apply to every nonprofit, not just universities. In my view, organizations should try not to compromise—in effect, applying a lower standard—to attract someone in an area they happen to need at the moment. In principle, it might be appealing to add a particular expertise or launch a specific initiative. But in practice, the result will be disappointing if implemented by the wrong person. At any nonprofit—from hospitals to humanitarian organizations—the quality of "the what" depends on "the who."

"The what" also is likely to change over time, and a nonprofit needs employees who can adapt. "If people join the bus primarily because of where it is going," Jim Collins observed in *Good to Great*, "what happens if you get ten miles down the road and you need to change direction? You've got a problem." This problem can be especially acute at nonprofits. If colleagues signed up for a particular mission—or, for that matter, a specific way to advance it—they might be especially inflexible about changing it, even when change is overdue. Instead, the ideal colleague is passionate about the mission but flexible about how to pursue it. Admittedly, though, this quality is not always easy to find.

For many reasons, then, finding the right candidate can be hard. If in doubt, wait for a better one. When I started as dean, we needed an expert in a particular field, but the candidates we most wanted were unavailable at the time. Instead of going further down our list, we decided to hold off. Fortunately, we didn't have to wait long. A couple of years later, we persuaded someone from our "wish list" to come to Columbia.

You can never go wrong by hiring the most capable and motivated people you can find. They will come up with new ways to add value. These self-motivated colleagues are likely to do this on their own, so they are easy to manage. They also can help attract other outstanding people, who will find it appealing to work with them.

Diversity

Diverse perspectives and backgrounds are valuable assets as well. "If you want the best decisions for any organization, you have to have fully diverse perspectives at the table," advised Kevin Washington. "If you don't have a diverse team, you will not get the best solutions."

Sometimes it takes extra effort to identify candidates who enhance an organization's diversity. The path of least resistance often is to find people through personal and professional networks. Yet this strategy poses a familiar risk: the candidates tend to have similar backgrounds, experience, and views as the people a nonprofit already has.

Just as nonprofits need to be rigorous in planning their programs—evaluating alternatives and going the extra mile to make the right choice—they need to bring the same energy and focus to recruiting.

As a law school dean, I was proud that our hiring committee was so thorough and demanding in evaluating potential recruits to the faculty. They were tireless in scrutinizing research and gathering intelligence on teaching and service.

We also tried to think "outside the box," adjusting our process to ensure that we were considering a sufficiently broad pool of talent. Which candidates could enhance the diversity of our faculty and administration in various ways? Had we gone the extra mile to find them? To make sure we could invest enough time and energy in this important recruiting effort (and in others as well), we made a structural change. Instead of one hiring committee for faculty, we decided to have two: one for veterans already working at other law schools and another for newcomers looking for their first teaching job. We also took the unusual step of approaching talented people who hadn't yet decided to become law professors or administrators. These and other creative strategies helped us hire a number of outstanding new colleagues, including ones who enhanced diversity within our faculty and administration.

Shaping the Right Structure and Culture

A well-run nonprofit is effective not just in hiring but also in allocating responsibilities. The division of labor should be clear but also flexible. "In a hierarchical not-for-profit, there often are a lot of layers of people," observed Carol Baldwin Moody of Legal Momentum, "and people don't feel the ability to make decisions." So Carol asked every employee to write a job description specifying "the things you would like to have permission to do without asking," while also urging colleagues to take on responsibilities not listed on it. "Ninety percent of what you do will be in your job description, but 10 percent is whatever needs to be done, whether it is going to the store or making a copy," she told them. "And that includes me too."

In assembling a team, nonprofits should strive to shape the right organizational culture. The Advancement Project looks for "early adapters" who are comfortable with change. "Society is changing so quickly and our movements are changing so quickly," explained CEO Judith Browne Dianis, "so we have to build out the culture and the muscle around the pivot."

DonorsChoose screens for humility. In interviews, former CEO Charles Best would ask candidates how they like to be acknowledged for good work. "If you have a very long and immediate answer to that question, that's a little scary," he said with a smile. "The best answer we got was from a candidate who said, 'I never really thought about that. I guess just an 'attaboy' every now and then would be cool.'"

Retaining and Training Talent

"It's not just about *hiring* the right people. It's also about *retaining* them," emphasized Rachel Garbow Monroe, the president and CEO of the Harry and Jeanette Weinberg Foundation. "You need to give them a path to grow and develop, so they can do different things over time."

To guide their development, effective feedback is essential. When Ruth Raskas came to JFNA from the for-profit sector, one of the things she missed the most was quarterly performance reviews. "It was just an obvious thing to me," she recalled, "and it felt uncomfortable for me not to have them."

When Ruth decided to kick off this practice at JFNA, her team was wary. "It was not a natural space for people to have that kind of experience," she recalled. "They got nervous at first. There was just a difference in culture."

To get them comfortable, Ruth explained why she valued the practice. "This, to me, is a way to sit down with people and say 'what's working well?' and 'what's not working?' and 'how do we work together to change the next quarter?'" she recalled. "I said to people that we spend most of our days on the dance floor but sometimes we've got to get up to the balcony to reflect on what's going on on the dance floor."

Before long, her colleagues saw the value of these conversations. "People were really appreciative afterwards," she remembered. "They said, 'Oh, this is a helpful thing to do.'"

Along with feedback and opportunities to grow, pay and working conditions are also important. Nonprofits usually offer lower pay than the for-profit sector, so they need to work harder to offer "a culture that is a joy to work in," emphasized Asha Curran, the CEO of GivingTuesday. Nonprofit professionals must "not feel like they are indentured servants who have to work with no flexibility and no attention to their lifestyle or their families," added Asha, who rejects the "idea that nonprofit workers should live in their parents' basement to have the honor of working at a nonprofit."

Just as nonprofits need to retain their best people, they also need to replace the weakest members of the team. "If you want to change the culture, change the people," a veteran nonprofit leader once told me.

"I've had people who have been rough on the organization," Judith Browne Dianis recalled. "They might have been great at what they did, but they've torn the organization apart."

Subpar work also is unacceptable. "It is demoralizing to the best employees to work with others who are disruptive or don't carry their weight," Rachel Garbow Monroe explained. "The most productive colleagues will wonder, 'Why are they still here?' It's important to fix that."

"THE WHAT": REIMAGINING GOALS AND PROGRAMS

Rigor is needed not just in assembling the right team but also in deciding what the team should do. As conditions change, nonprofits need to pivot constantly. "The only guarantee I can give you is that today will not look like yesterday," observed Wes Moore, governor of Maryland and former CEO of Robin Hood, "and tomorrow won't look like today."

150

In this ever-changing landscape, nonprofits need to respond rapidly and forcefully to new challenges. Thinking "outside the box," they should find new ways to pursue their mission. To maximize their impact, nonprofits ought to share innovations with others, prioritizing their mission over their brand. When a need becomes more urgent, they should double down on it. When a need fades in importance, they should pull back. If a goal is unattainable—at least in the near term—they should play defense instead of offense. In short, nonprofits should constantly reinvent the way they pursue their mission. Some examples of these pivots will make these points more concrete.

Same Mission, New Model

In the summer of 2012, Henry Timms, who was then the thirty-five-year-old chief innovation officer of 92NY in Manhattan, had an "out of the box" idea: a day focused on giving during the holiday season. As he explained to his colleague, Asha Curran, he wanted to call it "Giving Tuesday."

"Any idea that takes six words to explain is usually a good one," Henry recalled with a wry smile. "Black Friday, Cyber Monday, Giving Tuesday. It never took more than those six words to explain what we were up to." Asha was immediately struck by "the beauty and simplicity" of the idea: "Two days that are great for the retail sector," she recalled, "and a day that is great for the nonprofit sector."

Although Giving Tuesday fit well with 92NY's mission of building community, it advanced this mission in a dramatically different way. As a cultural and community center with a distinguished history, 92NY traditionally has offered classes, hosted talks and performances, and operated a gym, dance studio, and nursery school. "If 92Y had lived within its traditional model, and we wanted to engage in philanthropy, we would have organized lectures about philanthropy," Henry explained. "We've been doing that for 146 years. That essentially was the model of the institution. And we'd have convened some conferences about philanthropy, and we might have done some radio or some TV."

But instead, Henry and Asha imagined an entirely different way to advance 92NY's mission. "With Giving Tuesday," Henry explained, "we were trying to say, 'if this was the first day of 92Y, what sort of things would you do?'" They launched the first Giving Tuesday four months later on December 3, 2012.

Over the next few years, while Henry served as 92NY's CEO and Asha became 92NY's chief innovation officer, Giving Tuesday became a global phenomenon, which eventually was spun off into its own nonprofit (called GivingTuesday). On the tenth anniversary in 2022, thousands of nonprofits raised $3.1 billion in the United States alone, and the day was celebrated in eighty-five countries—in South America, Europe, Asia, Africa, and Australia—in countless languages by people of different religions who live in starkly divergent economic circumstances. When local leaders ask to lead a Giving Tuesday movement in another country, Asha and her team carefully vet them, ensuring that they have the necessary resources, commitment, and marketing capacity.

One of Giving Tuesday's great strengths is its flexibility. Each nonprofit is free to celebrate giving and kindness in its own way. In Liberia, an NGO replaced wedding pictures destroyed in a bloody civil war, providing wedding dresses and photographers. In Mexico, a daycare center invited donors to leave food, clothing, and other household items on "tables of solidarity." In Russia, where private philanthropy used to be conducted in secret during Communist rule, Giving Tuesday encouraged donors to go public in a "confession week."

"Generosity leads to all kinds of other good things," Asha observed, including "more empathy, more kindness, and more civic engagement." For example, when a small town in Brazil launched a Giving Tuesday campaign to renovate schools, children at these schools responded with their own campaign. "These children began a routine of regularly volunteering at homes for the elderly—cleaning, planting, singing, and reading poetry," Asha reported. "It was so empowering for these children to be in the position of helping others, rather than always being the ones in need of help."

To build on the success of Giving Tuesday, 92NY created an in-house incubator. According to its mission statement, the Belfer Center for Innovation & Social Impact "brings the mission of 92nd Street Y to the world" through "grassroots global initiatives, leadership programs and civic movements" that create "a vibrant worldwide community built around big ideas and doing good."

"The Y couldn't be prouder of its talk series. The things on stage are one of the crown jewels of the Y," Henry observed. "But that isn't our mission. The mission is never to put things on stage. It's to think about how you can create community and engage with the wider world. The world has changed a lot since the Y was founded in 1874. The question is, did we change with the world? This is always the question for nonprofits."

Mission Over Brand

The success of Giving Tuesday shows the importance not only of experimenting with novel ideas but also of putting the mission first—even ahead of the nonprofit's brand. Nonprofits exist to do good, not to claim credit. So if a nonprofit builds a better mousetrap, it should encourage others to use it instead of treating the innovation as proprietary.

This was Henry and Asha's strategy for Giving Tuesday. In encouraging others to launch Giving Tuesday campaigns, they did not ask for credit as the source of the idea; rather, they left 92NY off the Giving Tuesday logo. Henry and Asha realized that other organizations were less likely to participate if they had to acknowledge another nonprofit or if they could not reshape the idea to put their own stamp on it.

Why did others at 92NY endorse this altruistic approach? One reason was that "no one thought Giving Tuesday was going to work," Henry said (mostly) in jest. Another is that the head of 92NY's board at the time, Stuart Ellman, was a venture capitalist with expertise in innovation who saw the downside of aggressively branding Giving Tuesday as a 92NY initiative.

The strategy paid off handsomely for 92NY. "The great irony is that what appears to be a selfless act—not claiming credit for Giving Tuesday—ended up giving 92Y *so much more credit* because Giving Tuesday *scaled much more* than it would have done had we tried to own it," Henry explains. "So if we had created '92Y Giving Tuesday,' and insisted that everyone had to credit 92Y, the idea would have scaled within four blocks of the Y. It wouldn't have gone any further than that."

In 2019, 92NY took another institutionally generous step. Instead of continuing to manage the program itself, 92NY launched it as a separate nonprofit, GivingTuesday. Asha serves as CEO. The head of 92NY's board at the time of this spinoff, Laurence Belfer, joined the GivingTuesday board. (In the interests of full disclosure, I played a very minor role in this decision while serving on 92NY's Board.)

The success of Giving Tuesday demonstrates the power of sharing innovations instead of treating them as proprietary. A nonprofit can improve an idea and reach more people when other organizations offer feedback and experiment with variations. Indeed, an idea is more likely to become a social movement if it is "easily customized, remixed, and shaped by the participant," as Henry Timms and Jeremy Heimans have emphasized in their book, *New Power*.

Admittedly, nonprofits that invest time and effort to incubate an innovation may hesitate to share it. After all, a for-profit firm would never give away trade secrets to competitors. Instead, shouldn't nonprofits use the innovation to impress donors, showing that they are the "go-to" organization for their mission?

While this impulse is understandable, it should be resisted. At nonprofits, market share and reputation should be secondary. Instead, the burning question is how to advance the mission. If sharing an idea is the best way to do it, then that's what nonprofits should do. Indeed, that's what they *need* to do.

Doubling Down

Along with *sharing* successful ideas, nonprofits should also *invest more* in them. If something works, "double down" on it. At JDC, we ramped up our investment in a remarkable summer camp in Hungary, the JDC-Lauder International Youth Camp at Szarvas, which plays a critical role in reviving Jewish communities in Central and Eastern Europe. Before World War II, more than half of the world's Jews lived in this region. Yet between 1939 and 1990, Jewish communal life there all but disappeared under Nazi and then Communist rule.

Szarvas has played a key role in reviving Jewish life in the region. Young leaders have helped lead the way in this revival, and Szarvas has recruited a great many of them.

On my first visit to Szarvas, I met Tinatin Ciciszwili, who had come from Warsaw to help run one of the camp's two-week sessions. I asked if she came to Szarvas every year. "Every summer since I was six years old, except for the one summer when you didn't have room for me," Tinatin said with a smile. "I'm still angry about that." I asked if she spent the whole summer there. "I love Szarvas so much that I helped JDC launch another summer camp in Warsaw," she explained. "I am one of the camp directors in Warsaw, so I spend only two weeks at the mother ship"—that is, at Szarvas.

Like Tinatin, a whole generation of Jewish leaders in Central and Eastern Europe are Szarvas graduates. Indeed, when I was JDC's CEO, twenty-nine Jewish community centers in the region had senior managers who were Szarvas alums.

JDC generates this impact with only a modest investment—far less than it costs to operate a summer camp in the United States. The money would have been well spent even if the only payoff was a pleasant summer for children who otherwise could not afford summer camp. But in yielding a cohort of energetic, creative, and committed leaders, this has become a sensational investment.

This impact persuaded us to "double down" on Szarvas. I relied on JDC's capable regional director for Europe at the time, Diego Ornique, to develop a plan. An avid tennis player and a graduate of Oxford's Saïd Business School, Diego was constantly on airplanes, visiting JDC's work from Athens to Zagreb. A master at bringing complex institutions together, Diego has a unique gift for navigating cultural nuances and for thinking through the sequence of steps needed to achieve a challenging goal.

Harnessing these impressive skills, Diego and his team proposed a major renovation, as well as an endowment to make the camp a permanent feature of Jewish life in the region. To fund this ambitious plan, we worked with JDC's board to launch an $18 million fundraising campaign. Ambassador Ronald Lauder, a prominent philanthropist who partnered with JDC to launch Szarvas in 1990, provided a generous lead gift. Although we gave ourselves five years to raise this money, we hit our target in eighteen months.

Szarvas reminds me of the Duke of Wellington's observation that the Battle of Waterloo—the British victory over Napoleon—was "won on the playing fields of Eton," a highly regarded British school. In the same way, the Jewish future of Central and Eastern Europe is being shaped on the campus of Szarvas.

Pivoting Away From Lower Priorities

Nonprofits should pivot not only to ramp up promising initiatives but also to de-emphasize less impactful ones. At JDC, we made this choice in our community development work in the former Soviet Union. Instead of running programs in every place with a Jewish population, we focused on major cities.

This choice was rooted in an important demographic trend: most of the region's young Jewish people are moving to major cities. Younger generations benefit the most from youth programming, leadership training, and family retreats. Community development is a "long game" in which investments today pay off in later years. So we prioritized communities with large cohorts of young Jews, which will still have significant Jewish populations years from now. At the same time, we de-emphasized this work in aging communities while continuing to provide elder care, which was the most urgent communal need in these small- and medium-sized cities.

Admittedly, this sort of cost-benefit calculation isn't fun. But as tempting as it is to try to be everything to everyone, this isn't feasible. Instead, we need to focus on where we can do the most good.

In navigating these choppy waters, I was fortunate to have an exceedingly talented partner, Michal Frank, as JDC's regional director for the former Soviet Union during my time as CEO. A Hebrew-University-trained lawyer who worked in the Israeli prime minister's office before coming to JDC, Michal had a rare ability to combine compassion with analytical rigor. Her passion for serving JDC's clients was as adamant as it was obvious. To advance JDC's mission, she was willing to make hard choices.

Avoiding a Loss Is a Win

Another hard choice is to play "defense" instead of "offense"—something that doesn't always come naturally to idealists who gravitate to nonprofits. Yet sometimes the most important thing a nonprofit can do is avoid a setback.

This was a key objective for Ted Shaw, who led the NAACP Legal Defense and Education Fund (LDF) from 2004 to 2008 and spent twenty-three years at the organization. "We did a lot of work trying to protect the advances of the past," he recalled.

One of the nation's leading civil rights organizations, LDF brings court cases, seeking to set precedents that reshape the law. The quintessential example is *Brown v. Board of Education*, in which Thurgood Marshall, LDF's first director-counsel, persuaded the Supreme Court to end legally mandated segregation. Marshall went on to become the first Black justice on the U.S. Supreme Court.

To set the right precedents, LDF must be very selective about the cases it brings. The facts should be compelling so judges are more likely to agree. In addition, legal issues should be raised in the right order so each win strengthens LDF's argument in the next case. Conversely, there are risks in bringing a weak case. Every defeat sets a precedent, making the next case harder to win.

In mapping LDF's litigation strategy, Ted and his colleagues faced a new challenge: LDF no longer had the same influence over which issues—and, indeed, which cases—would be litigated. In an earlier era, the key cases were challenges to discriminatory government policies. As the injured parties, Black plaintiffs initiated these cases, relying on LDF (or other civil rights organizations) to represent them. As a result, these organizations could choose which policies to challenge and which clients to represent.

But as explicitly discriminatory government policies began to disappear, the focus of civil rights litigation shifted. The new disputes were about policies meant to *help* Black citizens, such as affirmative action. As a result, challenges to these policies were brought by white plaintiffs, who were suing employers and universities for rejecting or not promoting them. Although Black citizens had an important stake in these cases, they (and LDF) were not directly involved; in the language of lawyers, they were not "parties to the case." Rather, the parties defending affirmative action were employers and universities, who usually had their own lawyers, as well as interests and goals that sometimes diverged from those of LDF.

Yet if these institutions mounted ineffective defenses—or, for that matter, if they chose to litigate cases with weak facts—their losses would set precedents, which would adversely affect LDF's mission. "We were in a frustrating position," Ted recalled. "We had to invest a lot of energy in keeping the wrong cases out of court."

For example, in defending affirmative action, LDF wanted to justify this policy not only as a remedy for past discrimination but also as a way to promote diversity. Ted and his colleagues concluded that this diversity rationale was most likely to prevail in a case about university admissions, but they worried that the Supreme Court might reject it in a less favorable setting.

As a result, Ted was concerned when the Court agreed to take a case about layoffs instead of admissions. In *Taxman v. Board of Education of the Township of Piscataway*, the Piscataway school district had laid off a white high school teacher named Sharon Taxman, while retaining her Black colleague, Debra Williams. Although Williams had a master's degree and Taxman did not, the school board justified the layoff by citing Williams's contribution to diversity rather than her credentials. A federal appeals court in New Jersey sided with Taxman, rejecting the school board's diversity rationale for affirmative action. Against LDF's advice, the Piscataway school board asked the Supreme Court to review the case, and the Court agreed.

In response, Ted and his colleagues took an unusual step. They brokered an agreement to settle the case, so the Supreme Court would not decide it. The school board had already rehired Taxman, so the dispute was about whether she would receive back pay. Once LDF and a coalition of civil rights organizations agreed to fund two-thirds of Taxman's back pay and legal fees, Taxman and the school board agreed to the settlement.

Civil rights lawyers dream of winning cases, not of settling them to keep them out of court. "This wasn't necessarily how we wanted to spend our time and resources," Ted recalled. "The truth is, it was pretty frustrating, but you have to play the hand you are dealt."

Six years later, the Supreme Court eventually considered the issue in *Taxman*, but as Ted and his colleagues hoped, the case was about university admissions, not layoffs. In *Grutter v. Bollinger*, the Court endorsed the diversity rationale for affirmative action, holding "that the Law School has a compelling interest in attaining a diverse student body." The case considered the admissions policy of the University of Michigan Law School—a policy that Ted had helped to craft years earlier as a member of the Michigan faculty. While *Grutter* was not the Court's last word on the issue, the case confirmed Ted's judgment that the diversity rationale would carry particular weight in cases on higher education.

The lesson here is that nonprofits should be clear-eyed about what they can achieve. In some cases, the right choice is to play defense, instead of offense. Sometimes avoiding a loss is itself a meaningful win.

"THE HOW": CHANGING HOW YOU DO BUSINESS

When nonprofits look for ways to enhance their impact, they should focus not only on *what* they do but also on *how* they do it. Can they harness technology more effectively or use volunteers more strategically? Can they assign decisions to colleagues with the best information and incentives to make them? Are there ways to get more out of underutilized assets or to reduce costs? Again, examples of these various pivots will make these points more concrete.

Amplify Impact with Technology

With technology, nonprofits can reimagine how they do business, finding countless ways to improve quality and cut costs. Nonprofits should seize these opportunities, just as UJA-Federation of NY, the nation's largest Jewish federation, used technology to transform the food pantries it supports.

UJA worried about the limitations of traditional pantries. "There's a stigma associated with standing on a line in front of a food pantry," observed CEO Eric Goldstein. Traditional pantries also provide the same standard package to everyone instead of offering clients the dignity of choice. In addition, some clients do not eat particular foods because of health conditions, religious or moral convictions, or allergies. Frail clients also struggle to open certain types of packaging.

After conducting extensive research, UJA rolled out a better alternative: a digital choice food pantry. Clients order food through an online system, using a smartphone or computer. If they don't have access to this technology, a volunteer will come to their home with an iPad.

Clients can pick what they want, using an allocation of points based on the size of their family. "You don't get the same basket that everyone else gets," Eric observed. "You get the foods you want for your family." At the same time, the system incentivizes healthier food by charging fewer points for them. "Whole wheat pasta is fewer points than regular pasta," he explained, "and fruits are fewer points than cookies."

This new system, which UJA has implemented with the Met Council on Jewish Poverty and other partners, also avoids the stigma of waiting in line. "It's an online system that people can use from the comfort of their home," Eric explained. Clients can pick up their customized package of food at the pantry or have it delivered to their home. This ability to access food remotely turned out to be critical during the coronavirus pandemic, especially for elderly clients.

The digital choice system not only avoids stigma and offers easier access, but it also is more efficient, allowing UJA and its partners to reach many more people. For example, switching to the new digital system enabled a pantry in Queens to serve more than three times as many clients—34,524 in 2020 compared with only 9,288 in 2018.

Every nonprofit should look for ways to harness the power of technology. With the right pivot, a goal that seemed impossible yesterday may well be within reach tomorrow.

Amplify Impact with Volunteers

Nonprofits also can amplify their impact by using volunteers more strategically. This was how Leonard Leo and his colleagues turned The Federalist Society into a national movement whose influence is recognized on both sides of the political aisle. Indeed, a 2017 *New Yorker* article described the society as "the conservative pipeline to the Supreme Court."

To promote a conservative vision of the law, The Federalist Society runs activities for law students as well as for practicing lawyers. Leonard served as executive vice president for decades and then as co-chair of the board. When Leonard first joined the society's professional team in

1991, his job was to energize the lawyers division. "The student stuff is going really, really well," Leonard recalled hearing from Gene Meyer, the society's executive director, "but our lawyer stuff is kind of flat, and we're not really sure what to do about it."

"I discovered early on that there was a problem," Leonard recalled. "The model that we utilized for students just wasn't adaptable to lawyers." For students, it was enough to provide educational content on campus, but "lawyers are busy people.

"The old model was to get a bunch of lawyers to come to lunches and events, hear the speaker, get time together socially, and then they go back to their offices and their families, and do their thing," Leonard explained. "That's all well and good, but that's not going to create a movement."

Instead, Leonard wanted to "inspire and motivate our members to be citizen lawyers." He would help them find meaningful opportunities outside The Federalist Society. "We're going to help connect them to other people and other things," he explained, "that can make our conservative legal principles felt in the legal culture." For some, the right opportunity was pro bono litigation. For others, it was government service. For still others, it was advocacy in the media.

How could The Federalist Society match members with the right opportunities? "The key was to have a very, very good corps of volunteers," Leonard explained, "who really rolled up their sleeves and did work." The society relies on these volunteers to get to know other members, learning their strengths and interests, and then to "connect them to other people in the network who might have opportunities for them."

In principle, the society's professionals could try to play this matchmaking role on their own, but a nationwide network of volunteers broadens the society's reach. By including more people in the matchmaking process, the society increases the odds of connecting the right member with the right opportunity. An added bonus, of course, is that volunteers work for free.

"So let's say that one of your longtime chapter members becomes the attorney general of Texas," Leonard explained. "Well, he knows everybody. He picks up the phone and starts calling the buddies he used to see every month at the meetings. It starts happening organically, and that's the whole idea.

"We're conservatives who believe in the free market, so this is a marketplace," Leonard said. "We're not controlling it. We set the parameters, of course, and do quality control. But at the end of the day, the pipeline depends on the volunteers."

The Power of Incentives and Information

Nonprofits can improve their performance not only with technology and volunteers, but also with a better division of labor in making decisions. In determining who should make a particular decision, nonprofits should focus on two issues: information and incentives. Who has the relevant facts? Do they also have the right incentives to make the best choice? If not, how can we change their incentives? As the dean of Columbia's medical school, the Vagelos College of Physicians and Surgeons (VP&S), Lee Goldman produced remarkable results by using this approach in allocating two critical resources—labs and offices.

It is not surprising that Lee would focus on the information required to make a good decision. In pathbreaking research earlier in his career, he had identified the information needed to assess medical risks. As chronicled in *Blink* by Malcolm Gladwell, the "Goldman criteria" answer the question, "What does a doctor need to know about a patient with acute chest pain to predict the likelihood of a heart attack?"

When Lee became dean in 2006, he used a similar analytical approach to identify the key factors influencing the quality of a medical school. One of the most accurate predictors, he concluded, was the volume of research grants from the National Institutes of Health (NIH). By this measure, Columbia was losing ground to its competitors in the years before Lee became dean. "We were fourteenth," he recalled, "and we were closer to eighteenth than to thirteenth." To reverse this trend,

Lee needed two indispensable resources for new research initiatives—labs and offices—but very few were available.

"So I started with what turned out to be a fool's errand," Lee recalled. "I looked for more space." Labs were available in Westchester County, but this was a long way from the VP&S campus in northern Manhattan. No site was available near campus for a new research building. Even if one could be found, the cost would be quite high.

Fortunately, as Lee dug into the details, he realized something important. VP&S *actually had* a number of labs and offices that were either empty or underutilized. The problem was that various departments at VP&S had already claimed them, hoping eventually to use them for future hires. In other words, the space problem was not a shortage but a misallocation.

To prevent departments from hoarding unused offices, some colleagues suggested new standards, such as a minimum level of revenue per square foot. "If you don't meet the standard, then we can make you give up the space after some period of time," Lee recalled. "I looked at all those proposals, and I thought that they were very hard to operationalize."

Instead, Lee came up with a simpler and more radical solution: he started charging departments for the space they use for research. At the same time, Lee invited them to save money by returning some offices and labs to a central pool so others could rent them.

Since the departments need money to pay this rent, the dean's office began sharing more revenue with them. Notably, the departments still receive this money even if they use less space, so they have a financial incentive to take only what they need.

Lee's essential insight was that department chairs have the best information about both the space they require and the other demands on their budgets. Although they may well claim too much space when it is free, they are more restrained when they have to pay for it. As a result, Lee's new system assigns a key decision to the colleagues with the best information, while motivating them to make this choice thoughtfully and rigorously.

The results were impressive. During Lee's fourteen years as dean, his department chairs returned about 180,000 square feet of space to the central pool. That is as much as a large research building, which would have cost hundreds of millions of dollars to build. Although some funds were needed to renovate the returned space, Lee's new system still saved a great deal of money, which funded other key initiatives. For example, Lee recruited a number of new faculty members, whose grants helped move Columbia from fourteenth to fifth in NIH grants in the United States. Since quality tracks quantity, Columbia moved up to second in the United States in a prestigious ranking on the impact of its research. In short, a better method for making decisions led to a stronger school.

Getting More Value From Underutilized Assets

In allocating scarce resources, nonprofits also should look for "untapped strengths, and push off of them innovatively," explained Reynold Levy, who spent more than a decade as CEO of Lincoln Center, which houses the Metropolitan Opera, the New York Philharmonic, the New York City Ballet, and other performing arts organizations. "I have never encountered a worthy NGO devoid of underperforming attributes."

While the mission must always be the priority, advancing it in new ways that generate revenue has obvious advantages. For example, Reynold and his colleagues launched a consulting practice, Lincoln Center Global, to advise other performing arts centers around the world. They also upgraded Lincoln Center's restaurants. "In the twenty-first century, putting high quality work on a stage is not enough," Reynold recalled. "You need the opportunity for social discourse." Along with drawing larger audiences for performances, successful restaurants also yield revenue on their own. "We determined that if we presented great food at different price points in different places around the campus, we could make a significant amount of money," he said. "And we did."

Nonprofits also can rent out assets they need for their mission but do not use all the time. For instance, Lincoln Center's parking garage is meant for visitors who come for evening performances, but it rents spaces to commuters and shoppers during the day. Lincoln Center also earned millions of dollars, as well as favorable media coverage, by providing space for New York's Fashion Week.

While very few nonprofits can host Fashion Week, most have assets that are not always in use. Churches, synagogues, and mosques can rent out space when it is not used for religious services or other mission-relevant programming. Schools can rent their buildings to day camps during summer vacations. In providing revenue for the mission, these rentals are worth the effort as long as the asset remains available when the nonprofit needs it and oversight for the rental is not too onerous.

As the old saying goes, "every penny counts." As if to prove the point, Reynold and his colleagues even encouraged visitors to throw coins into Lincoln Center's fountains. All together, these coins totaled between $30,000 and $40,000 each year!

Transforming Costs Into Investments

Along with hunting for new sources of revenue, nonprofits need to control costs. While I was dean of Columbia Law School, one of our most important accomplishments was to turn a skyrocketing cost—the expense of housing faculty—into an investment opportunity.

The trajectory of New York City has had a profound impact on the school. When the city was facing hard times in the 1960s, '70s, and '80s, the school's reputation faded a bit. In 1963, four leading members of the faculty left for sunnier skies at Stanford. Nine year later, a prominent international law expert, Wolfgang Friedmann, was stabbed to death during a robbery not far from campus. Concerns about Columbia's neighborhood complicated efforts to recruit faculty and students. In addition, the law school campus was in poor condition, our faculty was aging, and students complained that the atmosphere was unfriendly.

Luckily, New York City's fortunes revived in the 1990s. A dramatic decline in the crime rate turned New York into the safest large city in the nation. Young people from all over the world flocked to New York, finding unique professional opportunities and savoring the city's energy, diversity, and dynamism.

This rising tide lifted Columbia Law School as well. Instead of coming to Columbia *despite* New York City, students and faculty regarded our location as a major draw. Capitalizing on this momentum, the deans who preceded me improved student morale, hired a number of new faculty (myself included), and upgraded our campus. The number of applications surged. By the time I became dean in 2004, Columbia regularly received more applications than any other law school.

To build on this progress, my top priority was to expand the faculty while keeping the student body constant. With a lower student-faculty ratio, we could offer a more innovative curriculum, cover more areas of expertise in our research, and promote closer ties between students and faculty. My alma mater, Yale Law School, has a uniquely low student-faculty ratio, and this quality has afforded the institution singular status and recognition. Yale spent over four decades as the number one law school in the *U.S. News & World Report* ranking (before withdrawing from the ranking in 2022).

I wanted to replicate Yale's low student-faculty ratio while also reinforcing one of Columbia's unique strengths: our faculty traditionally has focused more on "real world" problems than on abstract theory alone. I attribute this strength to our location in New York—a place where many of the world's foremost experts in law, business, and the nonprofit world practice their craft.

In implementing this vision, our greatest resource—New York City—was also our gravest challenge. On the one hand, the city offers access to leading lights of the bar and bench as well as unique opportunities to interact with the media. It also is a fun and exciting place to live. On the other hand, the cost of living is quite high. A law professor in Ann Arbor, Charlottesville, or New Haven can own a beautiful house, educate her children, and live comfortably on an academic salary.

But the same salary does not go nearly as far in Manhattan. Housing prices in New York kept setting records during my ten years as dean.

To increase the size of our faculty—and, for that matter, just to retain the outstanding faculty we already had—we needed to solve this problem. The most straightforward response, of course, was to offer much higher salaries. Faculty members could use the extra money to rent or buy the housing they wanted.

The main advantage of this approach was its simplicity. We could do what we had always done—pay salaries—but at a higher level. We would not have to design a new program or seek approval from the university to launch it.

But significantly increasing faculty pay had obvious disadvantages. These increases would put pressure on the law school's operating budget. In addition, the law school would not earn any financial return from this expense. In effect, the money would go out the door, never to return.

So we developed an alternative. Instead of increasing pay, the law school started investing alongside faculty members when they bought apartments. This had never been done before at Columbia, so we needed special approval from the university to do it. "This is a great idea," one of the decision makers responded. "Shouldn't the rest of the university do this too?" After that, we were "good to go."

This investment in housing enabled us to bring forty-one new faculty to the law school over ten years, replacing twenty-four colleagues who retired or left and adding another seventeen. To accommodate this 23 percent increase in the faculty's size, we had to add a floor of offices on top of our main building. Through this hiring, we built perhaps the strongest cohort of young law professors in the United States and also lured a number of distinguished senior faculty from other schools (including four from my alma mater, Yale Law School). We reduced the student-faculty ratio by 40 percent (from 11.5 to 1 to 7 to 1). Our new housing program was the fuel that powered this hiring.

Paring Infrastructure Costs

Whether the goal is hiring faculty or delivering social services, nonprofits should pursue it as cost-effectively as possible so their money goes further. Cutting costs is especially important when a nonprofit faces declines in funding.

This was a critical challenge for JDC while I was CEO. We knew we eventually would lose a key source of funding in the coming years: restitution from the German government for Holocaust survivors. This funding represented a meaningful share of JDC's budget while I was CEO, but it would be available only as long as survivors required care. The youngest were nearly seventy-five years old when I was CEO, with some passing away every year.

At first blush, it might seem as if a decline in restitution funds should not be an issue. Although JDC would have less funding, there also would be fewer survivors who needed our help. In other words, as the funding declined, the burden to provide care would ease as well.

Yet the challenge was that JDC would still have *other* elderly clients who were not survivors—they were born after World War II ended—and caring for them would become more difficult. The problem was that JDC had significant fixed costs in providing this care, including the expense of maintaining over one hundred welfare centers. These fixed costs were easier to bear with more clients. But when the number of clients shrank—and the German government stopped covering a portion of these fixed costs—our traditional way of providing care wouldn't be sustainable anymore.

But we couldn't turn our backs on these desperately poor clients, who had endured so much over the years. Without the care we provided, many would die. They had nowhere else to turn. So what were we going to do?

The answer was to provide care with a lighter footprint. We needed to figure out how to do this—and soon.

Regional Director Michal Frank and her dedicated team devoted countless hours to this goal, figuring out creative new care models. Instead of delivering food, we provided bank cards, which enabled clients to buy what they needed. To combat loneliness, we relied more on volunteers, as well as on call centers for clients in remote locations. We also cut the number of welfare centers almost in half (from 133 centers in 2016 to sixty-nine in 2019). When a center closed, its clients still received care, but supervision and back office functions were reassigned to other centers.

Even as we prepared to do without restitution funds someday, we did our best to maximize this support for as long as it was available. We wanted a significant increase in funding—even though our number of clients was declining as some passed away every year—because the remaining clients were more frail. As their health deteriorated, they needed more care.

I raised this issue with Greg Schneider, the capable and committed CEO of the Conference on Jewish Material Claims Against Germany (or "the Claims Conference"), a nonprofit that represents survivors in negotiations with Germany. Greg was sympathetic—he knew how needy our clients were—but he explained that the German government needed detailed evidence of our clients' needs.

I imagine that at some nonprofits, there is an easy way to get this evidence: clients constantly complain. To argue for more care, they offer documentation, which their service provider can use to make the case. In the United States, clients are not shy about complaining. As the old saying goes, "the squeaky wheel gets the grease."

But things are different in the former Soviet Union. After living for decades under Communist rule, our clients are more likely to think that "the squeaky wheel gets the Gulag." Even so, JDC's team in the former Soviet Union got the job done, offering evidence that was comprehensive, well documented, and compelling. Greg called me as soon as he saw it. Instead of saying "hello" and asking how I was doing, he began the conversation with only one word: "Wow."

Greg and his colleagues persuaded the German government to pay for more care. During my three years as CEO, restitution funding in the former Soviet Union increased by 64 percent (from $73 million in 2017 to $120 million in 2020), allowing us to provide better care to tens of thousands of Holocaust survivors. I am grateful to have been a part of this inspiring effort.

To sum up, successful nonprofits pivot constantly. To assemble the best possible team, they scramble to recruit and retain talent. As conditions change, they hunt for better ways to advance their mission, reacting quickly, thinking flexibly and expansively, doubling down on what is working, and shutting down what is not. They know when to play defense instead of offense. Along with "the what," successful nonprofits also reexamine "the how." They harness technology creatively, deploy volunteers effectively, and delegate decisions strategically. Tapping into new sources of revenue, while uncovering innovative ways to cut costs, they find ways to get the most for their money.

Remember:

- Nonprofits should constantly run experiments, looking for better ways to advance their mission.
- Since nonprofits rely so heavily on their professionals and volunteers, they need to keep looking for the right talent, find better ways to train them, experiment with different ways to divide responsibilities, tap diverse perspectives, and shape the right organizational culture.
- Just as some pivots focus on "the who," others should focus on "the what." Nonprofits should test different ways to advance their mission, sharing innovations with others, prioritizing their mission over their brand, doubling down on effective strategies, and phasing out work that is no longer a priority.
- Nonprofits should run experiments not only on *what* they do but also on *how* they do it. They should hunt for ways to harness technology more effectively, use volunteers more strategically, assign decisions to colleagues with the right information and incentives, get more out of underutilized assets, and reduce costs.

CHAPTER 8

PUBLICIZE

Share Ideas and Hold Yourself Accountable

WHEN BISHOP MICHAEL SAPORITO was hunting for better ways to engage his congregants at St. Helen's Parish in New Jersey, he picked up a book by two priests from another parish, the Church of the Nativity in Maryland. "I read it over three days," he recalled. "I was really busy—it was the busiest time of the year—but I just couldn't put it down. It was very, very engaging."

Bishop Michael also studied their website. "It was so good that at first I didn't think this could be a Catholic church," he recalled with a smile. "A typical church website has a mass schedule and an electronic version of the bulletin, but this was totally different. It explained who they were, what they were about, and how they engaged their community." Along with the content, the look of the website also was very different. "It wasn't just a bunch of printed information. There were blocks. There were pictures," he remembered. "It was really clean and fresh."

These innovations fired Bishop Michael's imagination. He was inspired not just to borrow some of their ideas but also to develop innovations of his own. "Their book really got me started," he recalled.

Sharing ideas and information is critical at nonprofits. This brings us to the fifth "P," which is "publicize": a nonprofit should post information on its website, explaining what it does and why.

"Transparency allows the field as a whole to be more efficient," explained Wes Moore, governor of Maryland and former CEO of the Robin Hood Foundation, which combats poverty in New York City. "I believe deeply in sharing knowledge about your work."

What information should a nonprofit share? To implement the fifth "P," a nonprofit should do something that few nonprofits actually do: every year, it should post a new plan with the main takeaways from its planning process. This "annual plan" should explain the nonprofit's priorities, strategy, and budget, offering evidence of impact and an analysis of costs. In addition, a nonprofit should explain its work in other ways, using expert reports, lectures, op-eds, videos, and other outreach through traditional and social media.

Fundraisers should constantly share these materials, handing them out like party favors at meetings and events. The annual plan also is a valuable resource for the fundraisers themselves. By mastering its details, they can make a more substantive case for the work. The priorities in the plan also tell them which programs to "sell."

Why should a nonprofit publicize the details of its work? This chapter offers four reasons—"the four Ms":

- **Mission**: By posting insights about what works (and what doesn't), a nonprofit helps other organizations learn from its experience.
- **Matching**: Publicizing the right information helps donors choose among different nonprofits so they can find the best match for their values and goals.
- **Motivation**: Transparency can motivate professionals and the board to deliver better results. Their work becomes more visible to professional peers, potential employers, friends, and others who matter to them.

- **Monitoring**: By sharing key information, a nonprofit mobilizes donors, rating agencies, and the media to monitor its work more effectively.

Sharing information is important when nonprofits are well run and even more so when they are not. For professionals and board members who are motivated and capable, publicizing the details of their work adds value through the first two "M"s: other nonprofits learn from their experience (mission) and donors make better informed decisions (matching). In contrast, when professionals and board members are out for themselves or not as talented, posting this information imposes discipline through the third and fourth "M"s, spurring nonprofits to do better (motivation) and empowering others to assess their performance (monitoring).

ACCURACY

Before digging into the benefits of sharing information, a key condition should be emphasized: the posted information needs to be accurate.

The Importance of Accuracy

Indeed, when the posted information is false or misleading, the benefits from the four "M"s won't materialize. If a nonprofit overstates the effectiveness of its strategy, others might adopt it even if a different approach would be better (undercutting the "mission" goal). By pretending to do work it doesn't actually do, a nonprofit might lure a donor into supporting the wrong nonprofit (undercutting "matching"). If a nonprofit can get away with exaggerating its impact and cost effectiveness, it is under less pressure to deliver actual results (undercutting "motivation"). Indeed, major donors, rating agencies, and the media can't monitor a nonprofit effectively without accurate information (undercutting "monitoring").

So sharing information is not a silver bullet. Unfortunately, the same problems that lead a nonprofit astray might also keep it from sharing the right information. Someone who is willing to make self-interested choices about *programs* might also make them about *disclosure*, seeking to obscure lackluster results and true motivations.

Incentives to Be Accurate

But the good news is that even when it is tempting to lie, there are compelling reasons not to do it. For one thing, telling the truth is a moral imperative for many people. This is especially true at nonprofits, where principle and idealism are such important motivations.

Even if some are willing to lie, others may well step in to stop them. For example, when one professional gives inaccurate information to a donor or reporter, a concerned colleague can follow up to set the record straight. Sometimes these corrections are made quietly or even anonymously, while other times they are offered openly and loudly.

Integrity is the most important motive for correcting a misstatement, but it's not the only one. Sometimes the motivation is self-interest or even spite. One way to undercut a rival or avenge a slight is to expose someone as a liar. Ironically, when this happens, one type of dysfunction at nonprofits (infighting) prevents another (dishonesty).

At the same time, reporters and critics have a professional duty, reinforced by their own personal interest, to uncover misstatements. For them, it can be a real coup to catch someone in a lie.

Just as self-interest can cause a misstatement to be exposed, it also can prevent it in the first place. A reputation for honesty is extremely valuable. Building this reputation takes years, but a single lie can destroy it. For example, if a nonprofit misleads a donor, it risks alienating not just that individual, but also anyone else who hears about the lie.

In some cases, misinformation also can trigger legal liability. Lying to secure donations is fraud. Donors might bring a lawsuit to get their money back. At a minimum, this sort of lawsuit is likely to generate damaging publicity, which can cripple a nonprofit and harm the reputations of professionals and volunteers who are accused of lying. In extreme cases, they can even be prosecuted. Faced with these various risks, even someone who is not morally committed to telling the truth has self-interested reasons to do it anyway.

Admittedly, not every exaggeration leads to these dire consequences. Just as for-profit firms are allowed to "puff" when they advertise, a nonprofit can use flowery language and strong adjectives. It is free to describe its staff as "supremely talented" and "the finest in the world," even when no one (except perhaps the staff's parents) really believes this. Likewise, a nonprofit can exaggerate its accomplishments, as long as it keeps its claims vague. After all, when a nonprofit says it is "changing the world" or "building a brighter future," everyone knows not to interpret this language literally.

But more specific claims are supposed to be accurate. For example, although a nonprofit can use rhetoric to tout its efficiency—calling itself "lean and mean," even if it really is bloated and toothless—it cannot claim to spend only one hundred dollars per client to solve a problem when the actual cost is five hundred dollars. Instead of puffery, this is misinformation, which can shred a nonprofit's credibility and even expose it to liability.

So when nonprofits post information—and, for that matter, when potential donors and other audiences evaluate it—details are helpful. Not only are specifics always more persuasive than vague generalizations, but details also make the case more believable (if only because a nonprofit can't just explain away inaccuracies as puffery).

To make the information they share even more credible, nonprofits can ask independent experts to verify it. Just as auditors review financial information, other experts can evaluate programs. For example, United Way of Metropolitan Dallas contracts with the Parkland Center for Clinical Innovation, a national research institute, to assess the impact of United Way's work. "No longer is it United Way saying 'look what we have accomplished,'" explained CEO Jennifer Sampson. "It is an objective third party evaluating our performance."

Admittedly, there is a risk that some experts might offer too generous an assessment, currying favor with a nonprofit so they will be hired again. But experts actually have a self-interested reason *not* to exaggerate in this way. They need to protect their credibility. If they develop a reputation for puffing, a favorable assessment from them doesn't mean as much. So why would anyone hire them?

As a further safeguard, a nonprofit doesn't have to hire the experts itself; instead, it can rely on one of its donors (such as a respected foundation) to hire them. As long as the donor—not the nonprofit—is responsible for deciding whether to hire them again, experts feel less pressure to please the organization they are supposed to evaluate.

To sum up, there are a range of ways to enhance the credibility of information from a nonprofit. This is critical because the benefits of sharing information do not arise if it is false or misleading.

Now let's turn to those benefits. Why should nonprofits post information? The "four Ms" are mission, matching, motivation, and monitoring.

MISSION

At some organizations, the need to share information is obvious. Educating the public lies at the core of their mission. For instance, the American Museum of Natural History's mission is "to discover, interpret and disseminate," explained Ellen Futter, who served as the museum's president for thirty years. Likewise, public libraries circulate books, universities and think tanks publish research, and nonprofit media outlets report the news.

Educating the public is critical also at advocacy organizations. For example, to combat racism and champion the interests of people of color, the Advancement Project relies on publicity and grassroots advocacy, along with litigation. "We give communications support," explained CEO Judith Browne Dianis, "because we have to win hearts and minds on racial justice issues." When the mission is to educate and influence, the need to post information is obvious.

Yet the focus here is on posting a different type of information—not about the *cause itself* but about the nonprofit's *strategy for advancing* it. For example, an environmental organization should spread the word not only about climate change, but also about its own efforts to address this issue. Why does it spend X dollars on litigation, Y dollars on grass-roots organization, and Z dollars on research? Which initiatives have had the most impact? How much do they cost?

Sharing these insights can help other nonprofits do better work. This is another way to advance the mission, so the first "M"—the first benefit of publicizing the details of the work—is "mission."

Should Nonprofits Help Each Other?

Before exploring *how* sharing information can help other nonprofits, it is worth questioning *whether* a nonprofit should help them. Aren't they competitors? By analogy, a for-profit firm is supposed to outcompete other companies, not help them.

In this spirit, when Robin Hood distributed clean needles to slow the spread of HIV, should it have stopped others from following its lead? When 92NY first launched Giving Tuesday as a day of giving at the beginning of the holiday shopping season, should it have kept other nonprofits from raising money the same way?

Obviously not. When it comes to doing good work, the more, the merrier! Unlike for-profit firms, nonprofits should focus on their mission, not their market share. Sometimes the best way to advance the mission is to help other organizations improve.

Admittedly, this is not always the case. Sometimes nonprofits need to keep secrets. When a humanitarian organization wants to rescue a group from persecution, they can't share their evacuation plan. Likewise, advocacy organizations often are tight-lipped about their litigation strategy so their adversaries don't know what to expect. Nonprofits also don't usually share their donor lists, since they want to protect donor privacy and avoid losing donors to other organizations. But aside from the rare circumstance when publicizing ideas or information makes them less valuable, nonprofits should do their best to share what they know.

This does not always come naturally. Some professionals and boards worry about losing their competitive edge. But if anything, helping other organizations makes a nonprofit *even more competitive*, magnifying its impact and offering a strong selling point to donors: by supporting one organization, they can help others too.

The bottom line is that a nonprofit should, indeed, try to help other organizations. How does posting information advance this goal?

Sharing Information and Good Ideas

For one thing, when a nonprofit collects useful data, sharing it helps other nonprofits make more informed decisions. For example, when Robin Hood monitors poverty in New York, it always posts the results. By following "about 4,000 families who were either in or right on the cusp of poverty," explained former CEO Wes Moore, Robin Hood offers "a really clear snapshot analysis of trends." This ongoing study with Columbia University is supposed to help everyone—not just Robin Hood's own experts—find better ways to combat poverty.

By sharing data with each other, nonprofits can disseminate best practices and help other nonprofits make better decisions. This was one of Ruth Raskas's goals at JFNA, an umbrella organization that supports local Jewish federations. She wanted to help federations analyze data on key issues and share it with each other.

"It was not without roadblocks," she said with a smile. "A lot of people said to me, 'you're crazy for wanting to do this, and no one is ever going to share data.'" But Ruth was undaunted. She knew how much value this initiative would add. "Big data has such potential for transformation."

She and her "small but mighty" team started with fundraising "because it's quantitative and it's easy." Which donors should a federation target? How should they allocate their fundraisers' time? Which efforts were most successful? The data showed patterns, which were evident in all federations—large and small—that participated in this project. The similarities were striking, and no one would have known about them if the federations had not shared data with each other. "It was clear that once you have that data, there are ways to rethink your own operations and how to shape them."

The next step was to share data on grants. As a pilot project, Ruth and her colleagues decided to focus on grants made overseas. "Here are the topics we are focused on percentage-wise," she explained, "and here are the organizations we are focused on percentage-wise, and here are the breakdowns." Once each federation knew what others were doing, they could make more informed choices. "It could be taken back to a local table," she continued, "so we could see what was going on nationally and think ourselves about how to optimize performance."

Once the leaders of these federations saw how valuable this information was, they were more comfortable sharing data with each other. Indeed, they wanted more! "We were at the point where we had more demand than we had supply for our services," Ruth recalled. "We had so many federations coming to say, 'Can we join? We want to be a part of this. We want to understand.'"

Nonprofits can share ideas not only about what *they* do but also about what they think *others* should do. Providing this guidance was a cornerstone of United Way of Metropolitan Dallas's response to the coronavirus pandemic in 2020. They could not do everything themselves, so they posted a plan for others to implement.

"We utilized our strength and superpower—which is community needs assessment, coordination, and alignment—to identify challenges and solutions," explained CEO Jennifer Sampson. "We took all this work, our priorities and our grant reviews, and we lifted it up into a portal where other funders could see and use our research and analysis."

To pay for this plan, United Way helped launch a COVID-focused partnership called North Texas Cares. "It was a collaboration of over forty funders," Jennifer explained, "including community foundations, private foundations, and individuals who all wanted to do something." These funders invested more than $50 million in initiatives included in United Way's plan.

"Rarely does it happen that big funders come together. Too often, they compete instead of collaborating. We did the work to say, 'This is our assessment of community needs. And these are what we believe are the most effective and efficient investments. Will you join us?'" Jennifer recalled. "And we made big steps with collaborations that helped make our entire region stronger."

Warning Other Nonprofits about Failures

Nonprofits should share information not just about successes but also about failures, so other organizations can avoid (or at least rethink) approaches that did not pan out. "As a field, we spend a lot of money making mistakes we shouldn't have to make," Wes observed. "If we could be transparent about what didn't work, the field as a whole would be more efficient."

Admittedly, many professionals and boards worry that this information could hurt their reputations and fundraising. "Nonprofits are very guarded about our mistakes," Wes lamented. "Our websites are full of things that we invested in that are now changing the world, but what about the things we invested in that just didn't work?"

While the impulse to keep quiet about failures is understandable— indeed, I have felt it myself at times—it is misguided. Instead of sweeping failures under the rug, nonprofits should learn from them. Ideally, these lessons should be shared with other organizations. The upside of publicizing these insights is obvious.

Is the downside really so bad? Professionals and boards should not be embarrassed every time their idea doesn't work. Admittedly, some failures stem from laziness or incompetence—and those are embarrassing—but others are a mark of creativity and courage. After all, if an organization never fails at anything, its goals are not ambitious enough. By being too cautious, it is missing promising opportunities.

"Taking smart strategic risks," Jennifer observed, "is how you solve problems in new ways that have not been identified before."

In taking these risks, nonprofits constantly take two steps forward and one step back. Knowing the right way to step back is just as important, and perhaps even more important, as stepping forward. So why not share insights about both of these challenges?

Unfortunately, nonprofits often are less comfortable with risk than for-profit firms. "Venture capitalists know that a start-up is going to fail at first before it succeeds," observed Asha Curran, CEO of GivingTuesday, an organization spun off from 92NY to promote a day of giving across the globe. "Unfortunately, the nonprofit sector is exactly the opposite." Donors want a specific result, and nonprofits deliver it in the safest way—but not necessarily the best way—to make sure they don't lose the grant.

"We have to create a new culture within the sector where risk-taking is encouraged and failure is accepted—where trying to innovate does not imperil the existence of your organization," Asha urged. "Then we actually could see a nonprofit sector that is not only known to be full of do-gooders, but that is known to be full of innovators."

Which organizations are freest to take risks and offer insights about failed experiments? Their donors need to value risk-taking. In addition, their professionals and boards should be highly regarded so failures are not reflexively attributed to incompetence. These nonprofits can perform a valuable service by sharing lessons from failures.

Costs of Transparency

While sharing information can add significant value, it is not free. Time spent gathering data and preparing reports cannot be used for other things. For example, if school principals spend time sharing insights with other schools, they have less time for their own faculty and students. How should this trade-off be managed? Since there are different ways to advance the mission, a nonprofit needs to weigh the costs and benefits of each.

This brings us to a key question: how costly is it to post an annual plan? Or to share other information about a nonprofit's impact and cost effectiveness? The good news is that this cost is low as long as a non-profit is already generating this information to use internally.

This is something a nonprofit's professionals and board should do anyway. As chapter 4 emphasized, they should produce a detailed plan every year. Admittedly, this is a hard job, which diverts scarce resources from programs. But this effort pays for itself by deploying the rest of the budget more effectively.

Once a nonprofit has prepared this analysis for its planning process, sharing it with the public is not hard. Some tweaks are needed to make it more accessible to potential donors, rating agencies, the media, and other outsiders. The posted version needs more background and con-text. It should omit sensitive information, such as discussions of specific employees. Yet these edits usually are not a heavy lift.

To sum up, the (additional) cost of posting an annual plan is fairly modest, while the benefits can be substantial. Helping other nonprofits to improve is one benefit, but not the only one. As the old infomercials say, "but wait, there's more...." Along with "mission," there are three other "M"s—matching, motivation, and monitoring.

MATCHING

Transparency adds value in educating not just other nonprofits but also donors. They need to figure out which charities to support. Like picking a treat in a candy store, this choice can be bewildering, even overwhelming.

Finding the Best Fit

The options are essentially unlimited. There are 1.5 million nonprofits in the United States and countless others across the globe that pursue a host of different missions. Picking the mission is just the beginning, since there are so many different ways to pursue it. Some organizations provide services, while others engage in advocacy or research. Even when they do similar work, nonprofits vary in their priorities, mix of programs, geographical focus, and client base. As a result, organizations that initially seem almost indistinguishable can turn out to be quite different.

How can donors figure out which is the best fit? "It is important to show what differentiates you from others in a way that is compelling and accurate," urged Eric Goldstein, CEO of UJA-Federation of NY.

To help donors find the right cause, nonprofits should share granular information. "Donor engagement is not simply about the ask," Eric explained. "Donors need the opportunity to hear about your work."

To provide this detail, Eric sends a weekly email to UJA's donors, highlighting a specific issue or program. "My weekly message is designed to reflect the values of who we are," he explained. In deciding to send these emails, Eric drew on his pre-UJA experience as a lawyer representing corporate clients. "The weekly message," he said with a smile, "is essentially a weekly shareholder letter."

A nonprofit should share information not only to "sell" donors on the work, but also to avoid awkward misunderstandings. Otherwise, donors might end up supporting work they find unappealing or even offensive.

For example, the environmental movement is divided about nuclear power. Supporters value it as carbon-free energy, which does not contribute to climate change, while opponents worry about radiation and nuclear waste. If donors feel strongly about this issue, they need to know not just whether an organization is "green" but whether It is the *right kind* of green.

A misunderstanding can be bruising for the nonprofit as well as the donor. Even though the organization may receive some extra funding in the short run, it pays a price later. Dealing with disaffected donors is never easy. If they complain to other potential donors, the nonprofit could lose other gifts. The easiest way to avoid these misunderstandings is to share details about the work.

This transparency is good not just for nonprofits and their donors but also for society as whole. An informed decision usually is a smarter decision. This idea is familiar in the business world. The Securities Exchange Commission requires public companies to disclose earnings and other information to the public every quarter and to offer more detailed reports every year. This disclosure is supposed to steer investors to the most productive companies. The same insight applies at nonprofits. With the right information, donors can identify compelling needs, address them more effectively, and touch more lives.

JDC's Global Strategy for Programs

To reap these benefits of transparency, one of my first decisions at JDC was to start posting a detailed annual plan on our website, which explained our strategy for aiding vulnerable populations in seventy countries around the world. Offering key takeaways from our planning process, "JDC's Global Strategy for Programs" answered three questions about each major program—the same questions recommended in chapter 6 for setting priorities:

- How important is the problem we are targeting?
- How effective is our response?
- Are we the right organization to respond?

For a brief overview, readers could scan the executive summary, which was (a mercifully concise) four pages long. To learn more about a specific program, they could find it in the table of contents. Or to dig into the details of all of JDC's work, they could read all fifty pages.

Sharing these details was a change at JDC, which used to cultivate an aura of secrecy about its work. Instead of "we'd tell you but we'd have to kill you," the new message was, "here's what we do and why."

Since our strategy kept changing, we posted a new version every year. After we finished the first plan, some colleagues weren't expecting to do another so soon. "Aren't we just going to use last year's plan again?" one asked me. In fact, each version was very different because JDC was constantly responding to emerging needs, testing new ideas, and phasing out work that was no longer a priority.

Some veterans sounded a cautionary tone. "This might end up being a document that no one reads," one warned.

But fortunately, our "Global Strategy" was a hit. "This really raises the bar," the head of a major funder said. "We are sharing your plan with other grantees as a model." Indeed, some new donors said that the document—and the transparency it embodied—were key reasons why they decided to support us.

We quickly found another use for our "Global Strategy." It was a great resource when we hired a branding firm. We wanted a higher profile because, as Senator Joe Lieberman once joked with me, "JDC is the most important Jewish organization that you've never heard of."

Standing out is a challenge because there is an "alphabet soup" of Jewish organizations. Along with JDC, there also is JCC, JCRC, JCD, JDCC, and JDRC—not to mention ADL, AJC, CJP, JAFI, JCPA, JFN, JFNA, JNF, JTA, JTS, JUF, NCSEJ, NCSY, NFTY, OU, RZA, UJA, URJ, USY, ZOA, and many others. (Seriously, look it up!)

Distinguishing one acronym from another can be a challenge, at least for donors who are not deeply involved in Jewish philanthropy. (JDC also goes by two other names that are more distinctive—"the Joint Distribution Committee" or just "the Joint"—but both sound a bit like an organization that sells marijuana.) So although loyal supporters never forget what JDC does, the uninitiated have been known to confuse JDC with other charities.

To help JDC stand out more in this crowd, the branding firm was supposed to suggest themes that capture what is unique about JDC. To do this, a key step was to study "JDC's Global Strategy for Programs." After doing their research, they suggested a new theme that was very well received: "JDC has boots on the ground all over the world. They are resourceful people who get shit done." After changing "shit" to "stuff," we were off and running.

▓ MOTIVATION

The first two reasons for nonprofits to publicize the details of their work—sharing ideas (mission) and helping donors find the right cause (matching)—are ways for well-run nonprofits to add more value. But unfortunately, not every nonprofit is well-run. Some professionals and boards are out for themselves. Others mean well but still don't do a good job. This brings us to a third reason to share information: motivating nonprofits to do better work.

The Allure of a Sterling Reputation

Unfortunately, when professionals and board members think no one is watching, they are more tempted to shirk or make self-interested choices. But when their plans and results are visible to the world, the pressure is on.

Nonprofit professionals have compelling reasons to care what others think of their work. A sterling reputation can lead to job offers, promotions, and raises, while negative "buzz" limits their prospects and can even embarrass them in front of family and friends. What if their neighbors see negative coverage in the media? Or their children hear about it in school?

Board members are just as allergic to public criticism. Serving on a nonprofit board is an opportunity not only to advance their ideals but also to burnish their reputations. The goal is to be seen as leaders of their community, not failed stewards who are asleep at the switch. Avoiding this public stigma is a powerful motivator.

With their reputations on the line, professionals and boards are more motivated to produce a thorough and effective plan. Knowing that influential audiences will read it, they think through the details more carefully, consult more widely, and take greater care with the language.

They feel pressure to improve not just their document but also their work. Just as disclosing earnings motivates for-profit firms, posting results can have a similar effect on nonprofits. As chapter 6 explained, well-run nonprofits should track mission-specific metrics, as well as the number of beneficiaries they serve, their average spending per beneficiary, and changes in these numbers over time. By committing to share this information with the public, professionals and boards become even more motivated to deliver strong results. Producing dazzling numbers makes them look good!

The Right Information

Admittedly, though, transparency does not always improve the work; it can be counterproductive if progress is measured the wrong way. For example, what if a hospital tracks the number of patients it treats but not whether their health actually improves? To increase its patient count, it might discharge some patients too soon while turning away others whose conditions take longer to treat. In these situations, the inflated total might sound good, but it's actually not good at all.

The key, then, is for nonprofits to be transparent *about the right things*. As long as the information they share is a true indication of their progress, posting it presses professionals, volunteers, and boards to do a better job.

The Price of Not Sharing Information

Unfortunately, there is another reason, at least in principle, why transparency might not be an effective motivator: some professionals, volunteers, and boards *don't want* to be motivated. In theory, posting should keep them on their toes, but won't bad actors try to wriggle out of this responsibility? For example, if they want to make a self-interested choice, won't they try to hide their real motive? Won't they be reluctant to share any information that could expose it?

The short answer is "not necessarily," if only because they might pay a price for not sharing information. When the results are good, keeping quiet about them is a missed opportunity. Why not take credit? The harder question is whether to share bad results. The worry is that they might harm the nonprofit's reputation. But actually, *refusing to share results* can also be harmful. For one thing, if a nonprofit claims that it does not have this information, isn't this a sign that it is not well-run? Isn't a nonprofit supposed to track its results?

If it *does* have them, why not share them? The most likely reason is that the news is bad. This seems especially likely if a nonprofit has been willing to post good news in the past. Why is it suddenly unwilling to share information now? This selective refusal seems like an admission that things aren't going well.

So either way, declining to share results makes a bad impression. A nonprofit seems like it either doesn't have its act together or is hiding something. To avoid giving this impression, a nonprofit usually is better off just sharing the bad news.

Admittedly, some professionals and board members might be tempted to lie in this situation. They know they should say something, but there is nothing good to say. Couldn't they just say what they *wish* was true instead of what *actually* is true? Unfortunately, this impulse can lead to disaster. If caught in this lie, they would set back the cause (and their careers) far more than the bad news ever would. As the old adage goes, "The cover-up is worse than the crime." As a result, the pressure is still on to be transparent.

The bottom line is that sharing information can motivate professionals and boards to do better work. Some are happy to share details voluntarily, while others need to be pushed. Who will press them to post information? Who will prod them to deliver better results? This brings us to the fourth benefit of sharing information: monitoring.

MONITORING

When the results are unimpressive, senior professionals and boards are supposed to figure out what is wrong and fix it. Usually, they are very motivated to do this. But unfortunately, they sometimes are part of the problem. If they are stuck in their ways or just out for themselves, someone needs to push back.

Not everyone can play this monitoring role. To be effective, monitors have to be willing to dig into the details of the work, and their opinion has to carry weight with the nonprofit's leaders. Yet although motivation and influence are necessary, they are not sufficient. The other key ingredient of effective monitoring is information, which brings us to the final advantage of publicizing the details of the work. Along with the first three "M"s—mission, matching, and motivation—this step also mobilizes monitors.

This is why United Way of Metropolitan Dallas posts assessments of its work, which are prepared by independent evaluation experts. "Every year we report community impact attainment on scorecards," explained CEO Jennifer Sampson, "so we have a consistent track record of accountability and enhanced credibility."

Who is in the best position to use this sort of information? Who has the motivation and influence to hold a nonprofit's professionals and board accountable? Major donors are at the top of the list, while rating agencies and the media sometimes play this role as well.

Donors

Let's start with donors. They have an obvious reason to evaluate a nonprofit's choices and press for good results. They care about the mission. To make sure their gift advances it effectively, they need to know how their money is used.

Some are willing to put in the time to find out. An increasing number of donors practice effective altruism, using analysis and evidence to find the best ways to help people. Similarly, "venture philanthropists" treat donations as investments and play an active role in stewarding them. These data-driven donors want results, not flowery rhetoric or emotional anecdotes. If they don't like what they see, they press for changes. If they are still disappointed, they look for a different charity.

Admittedly, not every donor wants to evaluate nonprofits in this way. Some won't take the time. Others base philanthropic choices on friendship and emotion, not impact, so they are less interested in the details of the work.

Even so, at least some donors are motivated to serve as monitors. Do they have enough clout? To change the way a nonprofit does business, donors need to persuade, pressure, or replace the relevant professionals and board members.

This is rarely feasible for donors who give modestly. Since a nonprofit can afford to lose their gifts, there is less pressure to keep them happy. So if a modest donor questions a self-interested or unwise practice, the nonprofit's leaders can simply smile, thank them for their input, and keep doing what they have always done.

But ignoring major donors is costlier. Losing their gift means scaling back programs, laying off professionals, or finding other painful ways to save money. Declining fundraising totals also can tarnish the reputations of professionals and board members. To head off these problems, they pay close attention when a major donor complains.

This is even more true when the donor is an opinion leader. For example, when a well-respected foundation gives a grant, this "seal of approval" can inspire others to give. For the same reason, if the foundation withdraws its support, others might do the same. This sway over other donors gives a funder extra clout.

To use their influence constructively, major donors need to know enough about the mission to tell whether a nonprofit advances it effectively. While this is a stretch for some donors, it isn't for others. Professionally-run foundations usually have this expertise in-house, as do umbrella charities like United Way and Jewish federations. Other major donors hire philanthropic advisors, commission expert reports, or do their own research.

To be effective monitors, major donors also need other skills and insights, which many bring from their "day jobs." For example, those who run for-profit firms are old hands at setting priorities, measuring progress, and motivating colleagues. Other donors spend their days helping clients access financing, analyze their revenue and costs, implement financial controls, navigate legal regimes, or make their case through traditional and social media. Drawing on their own experience, these donors can assess whether a nonprofit is effective at these tasks and suggest ways to improve.

Yet even when major donors understand the work and know how to run an organization, they still need detailed information from the nonprofit so they can kick the tires and look under the hood. Knowing what a nonprofit *should* do is not enough. They have to evaluate what it is *actually* doing.

But a nonprofit is not legally required to share these details. In the United States, it usually files a tax return called "Form 990," which is easy to find on the internet, but this disclosure says very little about the work. Instead of offering details about programs, Form 990 focuses on finances and governance. Along with information about the budget and internal controls, it lists who is on the board and what senior professionals are paid. (Not surprisingly, some of the most avid readers of Form 990 are professionals who want to know their boss's salary and competitors who want to benchmark their pay scale.)

Since major donors can't rely on Form 990 to learn about the work, they sometimes ask for reports as a condition of their gift, but the quality of what they receive is uneven. Sometimes all they get is a short description of the program's purpose, a bit of background on its scope and history, and its total budget for the year. This is not enough.

To be effective monitors, donors need granular information, such as the specific goods and services funded by the gift, the number of beneficiaries served, the average cost of serving them, and how these numbers have changed over time. Ideally, a nonprofit also should offer evidence of impact, showing that the program is achieving its goals and is more effective than the alternatives.

Again, well-run nonprofits already run this analysis, since they need it to set priorities and experiment with new approaches. By making it public, they can empower others to monitor their progress, ask questions, and offer suggestions. This transparency engages donors while also gaining their confidence.

The point, of course, is to share information that the nonprofit *actually uses*, not to put on a show for donors. Carol Baldwin Moody, the CEO of Legal Momentum (one of the nation's leading women's rights organizations), worries that some nonprofits don't always use the data they collect. "It's all about metrics now, and I'm a numbers person, so I get it," she explained. "I say [to professionals at other nonprofits], 'so what did you do with that data?', and they say, 'well, we never really thought about what we should do with that data.' Some just don't know how to analyze it." This is a waste of everyone's time and money. Instead, the key is to collect only useful data and then to put it to work.

In this spirit, a nonprofit should be proactive about sharing information. It should not just wait for donors to ask questions, if only because they might ask the wrong ones. Many donors have only limited knowledge of the work. Professionals often fume about having to gather this irrelevant information, which does not help them (or anyone else) make better decisions.

So when donors ask for the wrong information, the right response is to figure out what they really want to know and suggest a better alternative. Legal Momentum faced this issue when a donor asked for data on its helpline. In this signature initiative, Legal Momentum offers basic legal advice over the phone. The goal is not just to offer guidance to callers but also to find "impact" cases, which can set favorable legal precedents. Finding these cases is critical because Carol's team can litigate only a limited number of cases each year, so they look for ones that not only help a single client but also establish a principle that matters to thousands of women. Initially, the donor thought that "the best metric is how many calls come in to the helpline," Carol recalled. "But I said, 'We are increasing the number of calls, but what you should really care about is how many calls we resolved and what impact cases we brought because of the helpline. Those are my two measures.'"

In my experience, the best way to head off requests for the *wrong* information is to post the *right* information on the website so it is available to everyone. A well-crafted annual plan answers the questions a donor should ask.

Preparing just one report, instead of different ones for each major donor, is also less work. By posting it online, the nonprofits often can avoid writing dozens of other reports, which request different information, do not use the same format, and are due at different times.

Preparing one report for everyone also presses a nonprofit to send a consistent message. Otherwise, opportunistic nonprofits could just tell individual donors what they want to hear. For instance, if every donor funds a different program, the nonprofit could send each one a separate report describing the donor's program as "the top priority." But a nonprofit can't play this game anymore once it posts a single report online. The claims in this report—about priorities or anything else—are visible to everyone, so the nonprofit can no longer say something different to each donor.

Of course, posting an annual plan is not a miracle cure. It won't turn every major donor into the perfect monitor. Some are too busy. Others don't want to rock the boat. Still others have a quirky or misguided take on the mission, so they press for the wrong changes. But fortunately, many donors want to push the nonprofit in the right direction. To help them play this role, a nonprofit needs to share detailed information about its work.

Rating Agencies

Publicizing these details also empowers another type of monitor: rating agencies, such as Charity Navigator, CharityWatch, GiveWell, and GuideStar. The job of these organizations is to evaluate nonprofits.

Their ratings can be quite influential. A favorable assessment burnishes the reputations of professionals and board members and can also persuade major donors to support the organization. Rating agencies can also affect the volume of small donations. While modest donors have little leverage on their own, they have a lot as a group, if only because their gifts add up. By influencing large numbers of these donors, rating agencies wield significant clout.

But again, motivation and influence are not enough. To be effective monitors, rating agencies also need the right information. Unfortunately, they rarely have it; instead of evaluating programs, most rating agencies rely on Form 990, which has very little information about the work.

So instead of determining how effectively a nonprofit advances its mission, most rating agencies focus on governance and finances. For example, Charity Navigator considers "accountability and transparency"—that is, "whether the charity follows best practices of governance and ethics, and whether the charity makes it easy for donors to find critical information about the organization."

To make this judgment, Charity Navigator asks whether any assets have been diverted in the past two years. It also gives credit for particular governance practices, such as audited financials, an independent board, whistleblower protections, and a conflict of interest policy.

These practices are important, if only because corruption and conflicts of interest can keep a nonprofit from serving beneficiaries well. Nonprofits certainly need to cover these bases.

But covering them isn't enough, since good governance alone does not advance the mission. Along with strong internal controls, a nonprofit obviously also needs effective programs, and one does not automatically lead to the other. Auditing a nonprofit's financial statements does not ensure that it spends money wisely. Likewise, even independent boards sometimes make misguided decisions.

Recognizing that a rating should be based on more than just "accountability and transparency," Charity Navigator also considers "financial efficiency and capacity." It looks at a nonprofit's working capital, the growth in its budget, what it spends to raise money, how its assets compare with its liabilities, and the like. Again, these factors are important, but they don't tell the whole story. Even if a nonprofit has significant resources, it might not use them effectively.

To shed light on how a nonprofit spends money, Charity Navigator and some other rating agencies use another metric: the percentage of the budget allocated to administration as opposed to programs. Although these "overhead ratios" are easy to compute with information in Form 990—presumably a key reason why they are used—they are not a reliable measure of quality.

For one thing, they are malleable. The line between "program" and "administration" is not always clear. Some nonprofits are more aggressive than others in classifying an expense as "program." For example, some treat marketing expenses as "education" instead of fundraising.

Along with this potential for manipulation, overhead ratios have an even more fundamental problem: some activities cost more to administer, but this does not make them less worthwhile.

For example, if an organization works in both Russia and Germany, its overhead ratio is likely to be higher in Russia, but there are two good reasons for this. First, wage rates are lower in Russia, so programs do not cost as much. Second, audits and internal controls need to be more rigorous there since the Russian government is less effective at policing corruption. This combination of steeper administrative expenses and leaner program costs yields a higher overhead ratio. In theory, the organization could bring down this ratio by skimping on internal controls in Russia. But this would be "penny wise, pound foolish," since laxer safeguards could trigger costly problems.

Like internal controls, other types of overhead also are worth the money. A rigorous planning process adds to overhead, but it pays for itself by improving programs and cutting costs. The same is true of revisiting priorities, experimenting with new approaches, sharing information—and, indeed, all of the "Six Ps" recommended in this book. These steps all increase overhead, but they are a mark of quality, not inefficiency. Good management costs money, but the money is well spent.

Even so, some nonprofits might still hesitate to implement the "Six Ps," worrying that a higher overhead ratio would hurt their rating. This example illustrates a more general problem with ratings. When they use flawed criteria, they encourage misguided choices, which help the rating more than the mission.

The key question, then, is whether rating agencies reward the right things. Unfortunately, although they should focus on a nonprofit's work, they generally don't. Again, the problem is that most of their information comes from Form 990, which barely discusses the nonprofit's impact and cost-effectiveness. But instead of settling for the data they happen to have, rating agencies should get the data they actually need. This is the lesson of an old joke:

> Late one night, a policeman sees a drunk looking for keys under a streetlight. The policeman helps him look, but they don't find anything. "Are you sure you lost them here under the streetlight?" the policeman asks. "No, I lost them in the park," the drunk replies. When the policeman asks the obvious question—"why look for them here?"—the drunk responds: "This is where the light is."

For rating agencies, the key to more informative evaluations is granular information about the work. This is another compelling reason for nonprofits to post an annual plan. By sharing these details, a nonprofit can empower rating agencies to be more effective monitors.

Media

Finally, sharing information also helps another watchdog: the press. Many journalists are motivated to monitor the nonprofit sector. Seeing themselves as guardians of the public interest, they expose abuses and chronicle key developments at important institutions. Nonprofits are newsworthy because they target high-profile problems, generate compelling human interest stories, and represent a meaningful share of the economy.

Covering the good, the bad, and the ugly, the press reports on major initiatives, new leaders, significant gifts, and, of course, scandals. These stories regularly appear in newspapers, TV, radio, blogs, trade publications, and other outlets.

Admittedly, some media outlets are more interested in attracting readers than in pressing nonprofits to do better work. Instead of innovations, they want to cover infighting. Instead of rigorous analysis, they traffic in gossip or parrot the party line. If they ever compare more than one nonprofit—a more ambitious story than many ever attempt—they don't dig deep enough to expose key differences.

Like flawed ratings, flawed media coverage can be counterproductive, pressuring nonprofits to make unwise choices. At law schools, the *U.S. News & World Report* ranking is a case in point. Its methodology overemphasizes some factors while leaving out others. Knowing what the rankings cover, law school administrators are tempted to "manage to the rankings." In 2022, these skewed incentives motivated several top law schools to stop sharing information with *U.S. News*.

For example, a common concern is the rankings' effect on admissions. Although the quality of students obviously is important, *U.S. News* evaluates them in a narrow way, asking only about college grades and standardized test scores. In response, many law school admissions offices overemphasize these quantifiable factors while giving short shrift to other predictors of success, such as letters of recommendation, college course load, extracurricular activities, work experience, military service, graduate degrees, and community service.

This is a long way of saying that some media outlets are better monitors than others. Some go the extra mile to convey an accurate and nuanced picture, while others don't. Either way, nonprofits can help journalists write better researched stories by posting the latest information about their work.

How much influence do these stories have? When a journalist praises effective work or criticizes unwise or self-interested choices, do professionals and boards pay attention?

Whenever there is a story, professionals and boards surely want to make a good impression. They know that favorable coverage enhances reputations and fuels donations, while critical stories can be damaging.

But does the prospect of media scrutiny cause them to run the nonprofit differently? Do reporters have influence not just on the day they happen to call, but every day? Do professionals and boards shy away from self-interested choices, worrying that their motives might be exposed? Are they more likely to take painful but necessary steps, knowing that the press will fault them if they don't?

The answer depends on whether they actually expect the press to cover these decisions. Some nonprofits receive a lot of attention in the media, so the goodwill of reporters is especially important to them. For better or worse, university administrators care about rankings. Likewise, museums and orchestras pay close attention to reviews. By influencing whether exhibits and performances draw a crowd, critics can turbocharge (or trash) careers while also determining whether a nonprofit sells enough tickets to cover its costs.

But at many organizations, stories in the media are few and far between. This coverage can feel almost like a lightning strike. When professionals and boards do not expect media coverage, they worry less about what a reporter would say. Instead, they focus on monitors with more immediate influence, such as major donors and rating agencies.

Whoever the monitors are at a particular nonprofit, pressure to impress them usually improves the work, but not always. Ultimately, the key question is whether monitors push for the right things. Will they challenge unwise or self-interested choices? Will they demand better results? Or will they push the nonprofit in the wrong direction?

While nothing is guaranteed, monitors are more likely to add value when they have the right information. Reviewing a nonprofit's annual plan helps them understand its goals and strategy so they can ask better follow-up questions, offer constructive feedback, and make more informed judgments. This sort of monitoring can bring out the best in nonprofits.

To sum up, the fifth "P," "publicize," urges nonprofits to post an annual plan, as well as details about their impact and cost-effectiveness. This transparency offers four benefits. The first two add value even at a well-run nonprofit: exporting good ideas (mission) and ensuring that donors are aligned with its goals (matching). The other two benefits are especially important at a less-effective nonprofit: pressuring professionals and boards to do better work (motivation) and mobilizing donors, rating agencies, and the media to question flawed choices and press for better results (monitoring). Through these "four Ms," sharing key information with the public helps nonprofits fulfill their potential and do more good in the world.

Remember:

- Sharing information adds value only if the information is true. Fortunately, nonprofit professionals and boards have a number of good reasons to be accurate.
- Nonprofits should post an annual plan on their websites, offering the key takeaways from their planning process.
- Sharing this information advances the mission by enabling others to replicate a nonprofit's successes and learn from its failures.
- Publicizing this plan also helps donors find nonprofits that share their values and goals.
- Posting the plan also motivates professionals and boards to craft a better document and, even more importantly, to deliver better results.
- Sharing these details also mobilizes major donors, rating agencies, and the media to monitor a nonprofit's work more effectively.

CHAPTER 9

PARTNER

Raise More Money by Involving Donors in the Work

WHILE DONORS CAN ADD value by monitoring a nonprofit's work, their main job is to provide funding. All nonprofits need money to advance their mission. How can they persuade donors to support their work?

This can be an uncomfortable subject. "I think eighty plus percent of the population sees sales in a for-profit context and fundraising in a nonprofit context as at some level kind of demeaning," explained Charles Best, the founder and former CEO of DonorsChoose, which raises $150 million annually for classroom projects at public schools. "They imagine someone needing to ingratiate themselves and that's just viscerally off-putting to a lot of people."

Yet this is the wrong way to think about fundraising. After all, a nonprofit offers donors a valuable service: the opportunity to advance their ideals. In this spirit, my friend Joe Shenker, a Columbia Law School graduate who served for over a decade as chair of Sullivan & Cromwell LLP, one of the world's most prominent law firms, would always say the same gracious words when making a gift to the law school: "Thank you for the opportunity."

In my experience, donors are especially enthusiastic about a philan-thropic opportunity when they feel a personal connection to the work. The more they feel like partners in the mission, the more generous they will be.

Forging this connection was one of Charles's goals in launching DonorsChoose "We have a dual mission, which is not just to empower public school teachers in low-income communities and to confront racial and economic inequity in education in our particular way, but also to democratize philanthropy," Charles explained. "We want to let ordinary folks experience the joy of giving." To provide this satisfying experience, DonorsChoose is true to its name: it lets donors choose what they want to fund.

"A donor can express a personal passion and have a high likeli-hood of funding a project request that matches their passion," Charles explained. "Whether their passion is the book they read to their kid last night, the hobby that they pursue—yoga, gardening, knitting—the sport they played in high school, or the town where they grew up, they can express any of those aspects of their identity and probably find a project request that matches."

To help donors find this match, the DonorsChoose website lets them screen proposals for specific characteristics, such as geographic location, age of the students, type of project (technology, field trip, and the like), economic status of the school, and cost. "We have fil-ters on just about everything you might imagine," Charles explained. "You can look for projects that cost less than $500 created by Teach for America corps members who are working in Louisiana and are focused on history."

The donation is especially meaningful not only because donors can find the right fit but also because they form a personal tie to "their" project. "People come out of that experience having forged a connection with a classroom in a low-income community that has personality and that they feel deeply connected to, not just because of the proposal that the teacher wrote," Charles explained. They also receive "photographs of the project in action" as well as "thank-you letters from the students," which allow them to "encounter educational inequity in a personal way, rather than just reading statistics, white papers, or newspaper articles."

THE PRONOUN RULE AND FIVE "I"S

As the success of DonorsChoose shows, donors are more generous when they feel personally invested in the nonprofit's mission. "When that basket goes around, it can't seem like a black hole where you dump stuff into it and it doesn't go anywhere," explained Bishop Michael Saporito of the Archdiocese of Newark. "Donors need to understand the work and know that it was possible only *because of them*."

How can a nonprofit make donors feel as if its work is *their* work? For one thing, nonprofit professionals and volunteers should follow what I call "the pronoun rule": never use the first-person. The message to donors should not be, "This is what *I* can do with your donation." Rather, the focus needs to be on the donor: "this is what *you* can do by partnering with us." This may seem like an obvious point, but it is one that many miss.

While "I" should never be used as a pronoun, several strategies beginning with the letter "I" are quite effective. This chapter highlights five ways for donors to feel personally invested in a nonprofit's success: inspiration, improvements, involvement, integration, and interests.

These ideas have served me well, doubling Columbia Law School's annual fundraising while I served as dean. Before I started, the school raised about $17 million each year in new cash and pledges. In contrast, we raised a total of $353 million during my ten years as dean— an annual average of $35.3 million that was more than twice what the school had raised before. We attracted this additional funding even though my ten years as dean included the financial crisis of 2008, which hit the legal profession especially hard and really hurt our fundraising for two of my ten years as dean.

Even so, our fundraising success was broad-based. We received 121 gifts of $500,000 or more during my years as dean. Of these, ninety-two (or 76 percent) came from donors who either had never given a gift or had given much more modestly before.

How did we attract this new support? Each donor was different, so there was no "one-size-fits-all" answer. Rather, the key was to figure out which of the five "I"s in this chapter—or, more likely, which combination of them—was right for each donor. While the specifics varied, the goal was always the same: to treat donors like partners instead of cash machines.

INSPIRATION

Donors feel more invested when they see the work firsthand. There is no substitute for interacting with people the nonprofit serves, speaking with frontline professionals and volunteers, and experiencing the challenges and progress for themselves.

As a law school dean, I saw that when graduates return to campus, they were usually hooked. Interacting with students and faculty is a powerful reminder of the value of the school's work—more powerful than any video, brochure, or PowerPoint presentation can ever be.

Before I became dean, the school used to hold reunions at posh restaurants in midtown Manhattan. But our very capable head of development, Bruno Santonocito, realized that this was a missed opportunity. Graduates could always meet at a restaurant on their own. Seeing each other on campus, by contrast, was a more unique and meaningful experience. So Bruno and his team started holding reunions at the law school. The feedback was uniformly enthusiastic, and attendance tripled in two years.

If anything, seeing the work is even more critical at a humanitarian organization. As president of the International Rescue Committee (IRC), Reynold Levy constantly brought donors to see the IRC's work across the globe. "I was notorious for taking human luggage with me in the form of trustees and donors," he quipped. They were moved to meet the IRC's clients, whose lives and livelihoods had been shattered by conflicts and natural disasters.

The poignant meetings and spartan conditions on these trips nurtured friendships along with a deeper commitment to the cause. For these groups of professionals and donors, sometimes the healthiest way to cope was with humor. For example, on a trip to Kenya, Reynold recalled a trustee coming into his dusty tent at midnight to joke about the lack of creature comforts at their campsite. "I have figured it out. You said you want to transform the trustees group at the IRC," the trustee jested, "Could you do me a favor when you get home? If I don't make it back, please tell my wife why you designated me to be the first to go."

Bringing donors to the field was critical at JDC as well. For example, the first time I visited Szarvas, JDC's summer camp in Eastern Europe (discussed in chapter 7), I invited Eric Goldstein, the leader of UJA-Federation of NY, which is one of JDC's most generous funders. This also was Eric's first visit. He had heard from others about the camp's central role in reviving Jewish life in the region, but there is no substitute for spending time with campers and the program's dynamic leaders.

After we returned, I called Eric for advice about the camp. "For years, I've been hearing about Szarvas—that the camp works miracles, and that I needed to see it for myself," he said. "To be honest, given all of this hype, I knew I was going to be disappointed. The only question was *how* disappointed." He paused, leaving me to wonder what he would say next. "So you can imagine my surprise," Eric said with a smile, "when the camp was *so much better* than I had heard!" In describing his trip in an email to thousands of UJA donors, Eric described Szarvas as "a slice of global Jewish community the likes of which I'd never seen before." Compelling work sells itself as long as donors go see it.

If it's not feasible to bring donors to the work, nonprofits should bring the work to them. For example, the Institute for Priestly Formation nurtures the spiritual development of priests. In raising money for this program, Father Richard Gabuzda faces a challenge. "People know what a hospital or soup kitchen is," he explained, "but they don't know what *we* do." In theory, visits to the program could educate them, but this isn't feasible; a regular stream of visitors can disrupt the solitude needed for the program. Instead, Father Rich holds prayer breakfasts for donors. This morning of silence and prayer shows them firsthand what participants do for weeks at a time.

Likewise, nonprofits can invite beneficiaries to offer compelling personal accounts. For example, to speak at an IRC gala in Silicon Valley, Reynold Levy recruited Andy Grove, who fled Hungary as a young man and went on to become CEO of Intel. Andy held up an old hearing aid, explaining that the IRC had purchased it for him shortly after he came to the United States. (He had scarlet fever as a child, which caused hearing loss.) "Andy told everyone that when he spoke to the social worker at the IRC, he had a chart with all the hearing aids you could buy and their features and prices," Reynold recalled. "He picked the one with the highest price, and the social worker was so impressed with the homework that he had done that she bought it for him. He kept it ever since." This sort of detail brings a nonprofit's work to life. "For the people who were there that night," Reynold said, "this was the embodiment of the refugee experience."

Even if donors can't see the work or speak with a beneficiary, the right video, image, or written material also can forge a connection to the cause. During my years as a law school dean, I would send an email to graduates every September with my remarks to the incoming class, and another in May with my commencement speech. Every time, I received hundreds of enthusiastic responses, reporting that the speeches brought back memories and made them feel more connected to the school. While they appreciated my discussions of the school's history, they especially liked the advice I shared with students, such as the following passage from my welcoming remarks in September 2008:

> Be sure to enjoy the company of your classmates. Your
> time with them at Columbia is just the beginning. For

the rest of your careers, you will travel a rarified path together at the pinnacle of the legal profession. You will be proud of their achievements. Someday, you will smile at the fun—even frivolous—memories you share with people who have become so prominent.

You have a priceless opportunity to learn from spectacularly talented peers, and to let them see you at your best. Your professional reputation begins now. Be sure you are remembered not only as exceptionally capable, but also as exceptionally decent.

While your professional life begins now, be sure your personal life does not end now. You will need to work hard in order to make the most of your talent, but you cannot, and should not, work all the time. A career is a marathon, not a sprint. Sometimes you will have to dig deep inside yourself to meet the challenges that life has thrown your way—both professional and personal—and you should keep a reserve of strength for those especially intense moments. You will weather these storms better, and you will also cherish the high moments all the more, if you have close friends and family to share them with you.

Remember that life is about more than work, just as happiness is about more than professional success. In my opinion, it's a good bet that you will attain both—and so I wish you great success and great happiness at Columbia Law School.

Along with seeing the work and connecting with beneficiaries, some donors also want data and analysis. For these donors, the fifth "P," "Publicize," is a key part of fundraising. To be inspired, they want to see evidence that *they personally* are making a difference.

These donors want "a very attractive portfolio of investments," explained Jennifer Sampson, CEO of United Way of Metropolitan Dallas, and a "track record of driving measurable impact in our focus areas." To tap the support of these more analytical donors, nonprofits need to "to punch up your strengths," she continued, "in a way that demonstrates that you can drive impact more effectively and efficiently in the most adverse of situations."

IMPROVEMENTS

To treat donors as partners, a nonprofit should make them feel not just *inspired*, but also *invested*. One way to nurture this feeling is to ask them to help improve the nonprofit's work. "We have to explain where we're going from here and what kind of things that we would like to do," Bishop Michael observed. "That produces givers who are partners in your mission."

If donors believe in a particular goal, they are all the more generous in advancing it. This is straightforward when a donor has positive views of a nonprofit. "Remember what we did for you," a fundraiser can say. "Help us to do it even better for others."

But obviously, this argument doesn't resonate with donors who have a more negative view. Asking them to "help us keep doing the wonderful things we do" just makes them angry. Instead, the only way to reach them is to acknowledge the problems and ask for help in fixing them.

Engaging disaffected donors was essential at Columbia Law School, since the school went through a difficult period during the 1960s, 1970s, and 1980s. The building was in disrepair. The neighborhood had a high crime rate. The faculty was aging, and many kept their distance from students. In this cold and impersonal environment, the message the school seemed to send was, "You are lucky to be here, so don't complain."

I heard countless anecdotes describing the law school as something to be endured, not savored. For example, when a graduate visited campus on a snowy day, he was reminded of a common winter pastime when he was a student in the 1980s: throwing snowballs at rats. Another recalled how his car was stolen—with all of his belongings—on his first day of law school. Still another remembered getting out at the wrong subway stop, walking through an unsafe area to get to campus, and encountering a Columbia security guard. "Did you get out at the wrong subway stop?" the guard berated him. "Don't ever, ever do that again!"

These sobering experiences discouraged many graduates from supporting the school. In an extreme example, many members of the class of 1982 signed what they called "the Pledge," committing never to make a gift to Columbia.

To make the case to disaffected graduates, I would start by asking them three questions. (Not the questions from chapter 6—three other ones. You can tell that I often think in threes.) "What did you think of the education you received?" They would always say very positive things, reflecting on the valuable lessons they had learned from a distinguished faculty. "Did the law school open doors for you?" Again, they would respond effusively, acknowledging the school's vital role in launching their careers. "What did you think of your classmates?" If anything, the answer was even more positive. "My classmates are amazing. I formed lifelong friendships in law school. We are still close." But before I could say another word, they would usually add, "But I still hated the law school!"

For these donors, gratitude and nostalgia would not inspire them to give. Instead, a different message was much more compelling. "We know you didn't have the experience you should have had. But look at how much has changed since your time at the school," we would say. "If you partner with us, you can change it even more."

These graduates marveled at the improvements in our neighborhood and buildings. They appreciated the warmer and more student-friendly atmosphere and valued the many innovative additions to our curriculum. "I wish *we'd* had classes in national security, venture capital, and climate change," they would say. With the fervor of the converted, they became enthusiastic—even passionate—about supporting this progress.

This was true of the Class of 1982. Many set aside "the Pledge," enabling their class to set a fundraising record: during their thirtieth reunion, their giving was more generous than the thirtieth reunion gifts of any of the classes before them. How did this happen? The first major donor in the class introduced me to two classmates, who each also eventually became major donors. This trio then helped engage other classmates. At the thirtieth reunion, one of their friends told me how pleased he was to make his first gift to the school, which was quite generous. "Technically, I pledged never to *write a check* to the law school," he joked, "so I paid by credit card instead."

The bottom line is that even skeptics can become passionate advocates as long as they agree with the nonprofit's strategy to improve. Again, the key is for donors to see the organization's goals as *their* goals. They need to feel like the nonprofit's partners.

In a similar way, Rabbi Aviad Bodner turned skeptics into staunch supporters when reviving the Stanton Street Shul on the Lower East Side of Manhattan. A once thriving synagogue, its membership had dwindled to only thirty families when Rabbi Bodner became their spiritual leader.

The hundred-year-old building desperately needed renovation. "In the winter, we had gas radiators," he recalled. "We actually had to light a match to turn them on—who knows if that was even legal?" The lighting was just as bad. "It constantly flickered because the electricity had not been upgraded in who knows how many years," he said. A new space was not an option, though, since the historic building "was also the draw for a lot of people."

Yet a major renovation required a significant investment of time and resources, which was a hard sell for an institution on the brink of failure. "Why sink so much money into the building, since we don't know if we're going to get anything out of it? Maybe this will be the last year," the Rabbi explained. "Is there a future? That was always the question."

Sadly, the synagogue faced a catch-22. On the one hand, the building had to be renovated so the synagogue could have a future. On the other hand, the synagogue had to have a future so the building could be renovated.

Facing this grave situation, Rabbi Bodner could not simply rely on nostalgia or gratitude to motivate philanthropy. Instead, like at Columbia Law School, he had to acknowledge the problems, show progress, and invite donors to help transform a historic institution.

This is precisely what he did. The key, he explained, was to help the congregation "imagine something different." With aggressive outreach, he recruited more people to come to the synagogue—nearly quadrupling the membership in five years from thirty to 115 families. This momentum "changed people's attitudes, and then they were willing to put money down. It's just a very different mindset," he explained. "Oh wait, we're not just this sad place that might not make it for another week. All of a sudden, we're a serious force in the neighborhood."

Rabbi Bodner also reached out to a former vice president of the synagogue who had become disaffected years earlier. As a new rabbi, he was able to reset this relationship, recruiting a key ally who eventually volunteered to lead the renovation.

"We redid everything," the Rabbi recalled. "The floors were done. The pews were done. The electricity was done. The lighting was done. The painting was done. It was all done."

At the end of this process, the synagogue no longer seemed "like a little charity case," Rabbi Bodner explained. "Everyone understood that we have something important to contribute to the world, and that it's worth supporting."

INVOLVEMENT

To treat donors like partners, a nonprofit should not just offer them opportunities to fund the right projects. It also should *involve* them. Some enjoy working with beneficiaries. Others like offering advice or expertise, while still others become powerful advocates for the organization, spreading the word about the work and urging others to support it.

Early on, I worried about overburdening people by asking them to do too much. Maybe they would burn out or see the series of requests as an imposition. But actually, the opposite is true. The more they do—and the more invested they feel—the more they *want* to do.

This often is true of volunteers, who start by contributing time and end up also contributing money. At Thread, which connects academically underperforming young people with supportive volunteers in Baltimore, a volunteer who invests hours every week with a high school student sees the power of the work firsthand and often decides to help in other ways as well. "Volunteers become donors and donors become volunteers," explained CEO Sarah Hemminger. "We have been very fortunate to have donors who are deeply integrated in our work and that has enabled us not just to sustain our program, but to grow."

The same is true at United Way of Metropolitan Dallas. Along with money, corporate sponsors also contribute their employees' time. For example, in an initiative called "Southern Dallas Thrives," PepsiCo and Frito-Lay help school children by providing not just cash and in-kind contributions but also advice about career paths, opening the students' eyes to new possibilities and explaining how to pursue their dreams. "This role modeling is inspirational and motivational," explained CEO Jennifer Sampson, "because you can't be what you can't see."

There is a similar synergy between donating time and money at Her Justice, which recruits volunteers from leading law firms to represent women in poverty. "Pro bono attorneys are eager and excited, and often will say that this is the reason they went to law school," explained Executive Director Amy Barasch. "They also can bring all the resources of their law firms to bear on the case."

While Amy and her professional staff handle some matters on their own, they reach far more clients by involving and supervising volunteers. "We provide extremely rich training and mentoring," Amy observed. "We also review pleadings and brainstorm strategy on cases." As volunteers get experience, they become more self-sufficient. "Suddenly we have a firm with a bank of ten attorneys," Amy explained, "and they are mentoring other lawyers and growing that knowledge within their firm."

With this model, Her Justice serves nearly 3,000 clients each year at no charge. Almost 90 percent of the budget comes from donated legal services. In addition, a significant percentage of the financial support comes from volunteers (and former volunteers), as well as their law firms. "You need to create ambassadors" for the work, Amy explained, "and we are lucky in that our volunteer attorneys are really good ambassadors."

Of course, not every donor is eager or well positioned to work with beneficiaries. Another way to engage them is to seek their opinion on key issues. As the old saying goes, "If you ask for money, you get advice. But if you ask for advice, you get money."

Consultations are especially important with board members, so they can discharge their fiduciary responsibilities. Yet there is another benefit as well: when board members feel like full partners in the work, they become even more committed and generous.

This is more likely when board meetings are lively conversations, with everyone weighing in. Board members should not have to listen passively as professionals (or fellow board members) drone on with endless PowerPoint presentations. This "show-and-tell" can be soul-crushingly dull. Instead, the agenda should engage the board with important and interesting issues, seeking input that taps their expertise and judgment.

Admittedly, board members often are not experts on the nonprofit's mission. Yet although they usually know less than nonprofit professionals about the work, they know more about other key issues, such as investments, risk management, financial controls, legal issues, personnel policies, and media relations. They often also have experience managing colleagues, juggling different responsibilities, and shaping an organization's culture—all pivotal issues at nonprofits. Instead of paying high-priced experts, nonprofits can rely on board members to offer this expertise free of charge. I like to joke with board members about their "large negative paychecks," since they devote significant time while also donating generously.

Even board members who are not experts in the mission can still offer valuable insights about the work. They just need to dig into the details. When nonprofits prepare a detailed plan, they empower board members to make informed judgments about the nonprofit's impact and cost-effectiveness.

At board meetings, I always do a deep dive on at least one issue about the work. I like to focus on hard questions, which have compelling arguments on both sides. The more difficult the issue, the more useful the board's input will be. To prepare them, it's a good idea to circulate a one page memo, which offers bullet points summing up the competing considerations. The key—as my old boss Ruth Bader Ginsburg used to say about judicial opinions—is to "get it right and keep it tight."

I judge the success of a meeting by the number of words I speak— the fewer the better. After I briefly introduce the issue, I expect board members to weigh in, offering different perspectives. I want them to be actively involved in thinking through the issue so we have the benefit of their thoughts. It also helps for them to feel invested in the choices we make.

In my experience, the board usually agrees with the professional team's recommendation. When they don't—perhaps because the board focuses on a consideration that professionals have either missed or underemphasized—the professionals benefit from hearing a different perspective and respond with useful adjustments. In that case, the board's feedback almost always improves the plan.

For a board to play this active role, it needs to be a manageable size. With twenty-five members, for instance, everyone can be informed, engaged, and committed. When the board is significantly larger, much of the work has to be done in committees.

While a large board allows a nonprofit to nurture a bigger group of committed and generous donors, there are other ways to accomplish this goal. For example, along with a fiduciary board, a nonprofit can also have advisory boards. These groups can also be consulted about key issues, using the same active format that successfully engages a fiduciary board.

This lesson applies not just to fiduciary boards and advisory groups but to all donors. The more input they give, the more generous they become. So instead of asking for help with a predetermined goal, the better approach is for donors to *help define* the goal. Human nature being what it is, people are more committed to ideas they help develop.

In this spirit, a meeting with a donor should be a conversation, not a presentation. Although the goal is to make the case for the nonprofit's work, the key points should flow organically in the conversation. Sharing the latest news makes donors feel like insiders. An effective fundraiser also finds opportunities to ask "what do you think?" or "what would you do?"

Again, some donors have less expertise on a nonprofit's mission than others. But their own professional expertise can add significant value. They also can still offer useful feedback about the work—even if they are not experts in the mission—as long as they are given the relevant information. I have regularly used donors as sounding boards. I shared knotty challenges with them, laying out the competing considerations and asking for their reaction. I almost always learned something in these conversations.

Donors of time and money can become more involved—and thus feel more like partners—not just by serving beneficiaries and giving advice but also by spreading the word. They can make the case to others to get involved.

One of the most effective ways to recruit new volunteers is through people who already are volunteering. "Looking back now, our early success in recruiting volunteers came from the fact that we actually weren't casting a wide net," explained Sarah Hemminger, co-founder and CEO of Thread, which connects students with volunteers. "Volunteers would recruit their friends."

For example, a small group of Johns Hopkins medical students brought a large group of classmates to one of Thread's first information sessions. "The reason they were able to recruit more than 120 people that day is because they were doing it from an existing social network of people through which they had credibility," Sarah recalled.

This has become a winning formula for Thread. "Existing social ties help build new, more diverse social ties that become foundational components," Sarah continued. "It creates a virtuous cycle. As Hopkins med students volunteer together in Thread, their relationships become even deeper because they have a shared goal outside of going to school together, and that pours back into their ability to collaborate and work together."

Just as volunteers are especially effective recruiters for other volunteers, donors are especially effective recruiters for other donors. "People give to institutions and causes they admire," explained Reynold Levy, who has served as CEO of the IRC, Lincoln Center, 92NY, and Robin Hood, "and they also give to people they respect and with whom they have a relationship." Someone who is giving generously has credibility in urging others to do so as well.

In seeking financial support for an extensive renovation of Lincoln Center, Reynold knew that board chairs and other generous donors were especially powerful advocates. Donors are particularly generous when approached by friends and colleagues they trust. "Hopefully they gave because they trusted that management knew what they were doing," Reynold explained. "But they also trusted [the renovation plan] because...the teams of trustees who would oversee this planning were also solicitors."

A donor who is not comfortable asking friends for money can still introduce them to nonprofit professionals, who can follow up with an ask. Donors also can authorize the nonprofit to mention their generosity to friends. When meeting potential donors, Reynold would bring a list reporting the donations of people they knew. "Man, they would hone in on that list," Reynold recalled. "After we left, they would call their friends or colleagues and ask what motivated them to give so generously."

Donors can use their networks not just to raise money but also to spread the word on social media. They can post content, such as videos, op-eds, and blog posts, encouraging friends to act on it, add their own commentary, and pass it on to others. Through this activism, everyone develops a greater sense of ownership in the cause.

In short, donors feel like partners when they do more than just give money. Some like to serve beneficiaries, while others want to give advice or raise money. These experiences reinforce their commitment. The more they do, the more they give.

INTEGRATION

Of course, personal ties are important as well. Many donors are motivated not only by inspiration, improvements, and involvement, but also by another "I": integration. For them, partnering with a nonprofit means joining a community. They forge friendships with nonprofit professionals, volunteers, beneficiaries, and other donors. When a nonprofit integrates them into a community grounded in shared values, interests, and experiences, these donors become even more committed.

Nurturing these ties is a key part of nonprofit leadership. "I spent a lot of time just having coffee with people, meeting with them, and inviting them over to our house," recalled Rabbi Aviad Bodner, explaining how he quadrupled the membership of the Stanton Street Shul in five years. "It was about creating a personal relationship between me and every person" in the synagogue.

Along with forming these ties themselves, nonprofit leaders also should nurture connections among others within the community. "I didn't see myself as the rabbi who's there just to write sermons, answer a lot of questions, and give advice," Rabbi Bodner explained. "I saw myself as a community organizer. I saw that to be my job."

How did he do it? "We worked a lot on food," he said with a wry smile. "We wanted to get people together, and we had to create meaningful relationships among our members." So he hosted a dinner at his home every Friday night (when the Jewish Sabbath begins), and the synagogue started having communal Friday night dinners once a month. "To build community, I realized that I had to learn how to deal with caterers," he joked. "In a way, I needed to be more like a party planner all of a sudden, instead of being a rabbi."

Reynold Levy had a similar insight as president of the IRC. "I never met a refugee who objected to getting an inoculation because the money came from donors who went to a Broadway show," he observed. "It's okay to have a little fun."

While serving as president of Lincoln Center, Reynold increased the number of galas from two to fifteen every year. Each of these events convened members of different professional communities; one was for hedge fund managers, another was for the tech industry, and the like. "My middle name is gala," Reynold quipped.

At large nonprofits, it becomes more difficult for leaders to form personal ties with everyone. A more practical alternative is to form smaller groups within the broader community, tasking professionals or volunteers to nurture them. For example, universities organize separate activities and fundraising campaigns for each graduating class, tapping class volunteers to lead these mini-communities. Likewise, United Way, Jewish federations, and other umbrella charities integrate donors into a community by inviting them to serve on committees, which decide how to allocate funds.

Houses of worship also can form sub-units within the congregation. As pastor of St. Helen's Church in Westfield, New Jersey, Bishop Michael Saporito understood the value of these small groups. "We were only two or three priests in a church with 4,300 families. That's 15,000 people," he explained. "How could you possibly know 4,300 families? How could you possibly know what's going on in people's lives? Well, the answer is that you can't."

Instead, he and his colleagues formed small groups so parishioners could build their own close-knit communities. "Small groups were a way that you could continue people's reflection upon what was going on," he explained. "On Sunday, you could gather them in small groups to continue their growth in faith."

These subgroups are effective at outreach. "Sometimes people have trouble going to the formal church first, but they might go to a group hosted by a friend or neighbor," Bishop Michael observed. "This is less threatening."

These groups also provide support when members face hard times. "As people talk about what's going on in their lives, others in the group become aware of who's hurting and who has a health issue—that sort of thing," he explained. "The group's right there and can offer prayerful support and help." The groups also are a "really good way of sharing information," he continued. "The parish leaders would find out that certain people are struggling and follow up with them."

Rabbi Aviad Bodner used a similar strategy when he moved to a larger congregation, Ramath Orah, on the Upper West Side of Manhattan. (In the interests of full disclosure, I am a member of the congregation.) "The idea was to have board members take on some of that responsibility because I can't have a touch point with 120 or 130 families," he explained. "But if every board member has contact with eight families, and I am in touch with the board members, then I can follow up to see how everyone's doing."

This network proved invaluable during the coronavirus pandemic. "Board members already were in touch with the members that they knew, so they could check in to make sure they have everything they need," he explained. "How are they feeling? Are they in quarantine? Can we help with groceries? I definitely didn't have this in mind in my wildest dreams (or, really, nightmares), but it worked out well."

To sum up, philanthropy can be turbocharged by personal ties. Donors feel more like partners when they forge personal relationships with a nonprofit's professionals, volunteers, beneficiaries, board, and donors. The more integrated they are in this community, the more committed and generous they become.

INTERESTS

Along with the first four "I"s—inspiration, improvements, involvement, and integration—there is a fifth: interests. To feel like partners, donors should have discretion to choose which initiatives they want to support.

This does not mean that donors should control a nonprofit's agenda. Rather, donors should pick from a menu of initiatives the nonprofit *already wants to run*. Although this choice is bounded, it can still nurture a sense of ownership. When donors start seeing a program as "their" program, they almost always become more generous.

Traditionally, charities such as United Way and Jewish federations have not offered donors this sort of discretion. These umbrella charities have mainly asked for "unrestricted" gifts, which can be spent however they choose. For example, United Way of Metropolitan Dallas used to be known as a "community chest that evaluated grants and made annual allocations to a set group of nonprofit organizations," explained CEO Jennifer Sampson. "We raised discretionary funding and could deploy this creative capital in areas we determined were the highest and best use."

Yet donors are increasingly unwilling to delegate these choices. "Many don't want to give to a grants process, even if it's a grants process that produces the very best investments against measurable goals," Jennifer observed. "That model doesn't work in the world we live in today like it did fifty years ago."

Attracting unrestricted gifts has become more difficult because donors—especially younger ones—want a more active role. "People want choice," Jennifer observed. "The younger workforce wants to engage and volunteer before they give." They also want to direct their donations. "What we've learned is that fewer and fewer funders say, 'Here's unrestricted funding to put through your mutual fund of nonprofit partners,'" she continued. "They want to address a specific problem or solve a specific challenge in measurable ways."

To reach these donors, nonprofits need to offer options. "We've moved into the business of community impact product development," Jennifer explained. "We offer our funders targeted initiatives and products in our focus areas, and we often build, architect, and co-create these interventions with our funders to address a very specific and measurable need." In short, United Way treats its funders as partners.

Even as a nonprofit offers donors this sort of active role, it has to steer clear of a problem emphasized earlier: "don't just follow the money." Nonprofits must not let fundraising dictate its priorities. Rather, to reap the benefits of the first and third "P"s, "plan" and "prioritize," a nonprofit needs to make sure that its mission and program priorities determine fundraising, not the other way around. Again, if a donor has a great idea, the nonprofit should be open to it. But when a donor wants to fund something that a nonprofit either does not prioritize or cannot do well, the right answer usually is to decline the gift. Otherwise, the nonprofit might deliver mediocre results, disappointing the donor, sapping the morale of professionals and volunteers, and tarnishing its reputation.

Admittedly, there is still a plausible reason to accept this sort of gift in some cases: recruiting new donors. The hope is that even if a donor's first gift is not for a high priority, the second or third one will be. To steer donors to something else later, a nonprofit needs to deliver strong results now. By investing in this low-priority initiative, the nonprofit hopefully engages a new donor.

Yet in my experience, this strategy fails more often than it succeeds. When donors are initially reluctant to support a nonprofit's core work, the reason sometimes is that they don't find it compelling—and maybe they never will. Once this lack of fit becomes clear, the nonprofit should cut its losses. Instead of renewing the grant, it should pull the plug on the low-priority initiative.

How can a nonprofit let donors make choices while still steering them to priority initiatives? The key is to seek targeted donations only for expenses *it already plans to bear*. After setting its budget with a rigorous planning process, a nonprofit should invite donors to cover any budget line that is not yet fully funded. In paying these expenses, donors follow the nonprofit's lead, allocating money where the nonprofit wants it to go. So although donors do make a choice, which encourages them to "own" the work, their targeted donations still leave a nonprofit with nearly as much discretion as unrestricted donations.

For example, assume that a college has a $100 million budget, which includes: $40 million for faculty salaries; $20 million for financial aid; $20 million for campus maintenance; $15 million for administrative salaries; and $5 million for athletics and extracurricular programs. It can fund 80 percent of its expenses through tuition and needs $20 million of donations to cover the rest.

In principle, the administration might want only unrestricted gifts so it has complete discretion to allocate these funds. But unrestricted donations have an obvious downside: donors cannot choose what they want to support. Since donors are less likely to forge a personal tie to the work, they often won't give as generously. This is a missed opportunity.

Instead, the college should invite donors to choose from a menu, consisting of the five categories of expenses in its budget. Since donors have different preferences, some will gravitate to financial aid, others to research and teaching, and still others to buildings and athletics. By sorting in this way, donors ensure that a range of needs are covered.

To encourage donors to "own" the initiative they select, the college should provide a detailed report. For example, if donors support financial aid, they should get information on the financial aid budget, the average award, the number of students receiving aid, and biographical information about a representative sample of students. Ideally, they also meet "their" students or receive a personal note from them.

Sophisticated donors understand that when they pick from a predetermined menu, they are *filling in* the nonprofit's budget, not *changing* it. Does this defeat the purpose? Does the limited nature of their choice keep them from feeling like partners in the work?

In my experience, the answer usually is "not at all." For example, donors to Columbia Law School are sophisticated lawyers who understand budgetary realities. In choosing among the options we offered, they often would say something like, "I know money is fungible, so my choice doesn't really affect the school." In fact, many took comfort in this, knowing that expert professionals had vetted the options and confirmed that each was valuable. They still weighed the options carefully. Most also developed a personal connection to "their" work. They wanted to meet the faculty they were funding, see the room they were renovating, or hear about (or even attend) the event they were supporting.

This is not to say that donors *never* try to change a nonprofit's budget and priorities. When this is their goal, they want their gifts to accomplish it. At Columbia Law School, for example, donors helped us do a number of things we had not done before, including more generous tuition forgiveness when graduates work in public interest law, a robust partnership with the business school, as well as new research centers on national security, climate change, and a dozen other cutting-edge topics. These gifts changed our budget, but they were for initiatives our faculty and students wanted to pursue.

This alignment of interests is critical. When donors are eager to change a nonprofit's budget and priorities, the crucial question is whether the nonprofit's board and professionals agree with the new direction. If they do—and often they are the ones suggesting it in the first place—they are happy to commit to the change.

Yet when a nonprofit does not want to change its priorities or mix of programs, it should be careful not to raise more for a specific need than it wants to spend. In our hypothetical example, the college plans to spend only $5 million on athletics and extracurricular activities. Once it hits this target, it needs to steer donors to other needs. Otherwise, there would be a surplus for student activities and a deficit for everything else.

One way to avoid this mismatch is to define options on the menu more broadly, leaving a measure of discretion to shift money where it is needed. For example, it is better to ask donors to fund "athletics" instead of a specific team. Otherwise, if the tennis team is especially popular, there could be too much for tennis and not enough for fencing and track. The college should still invite donors to express a preference but without committing to honor it in all cases. If donors choose different team, there is no issue. But if too many pick the same team, some of their gifts should go to this top choice, while the rest should support other teams.

Another familiar challenge with targeted donations is that some expenses are less appealing than others. For example, few donors leap to pay utility bills, postage, or legal fees. Instead of covering these indirect costs, donors usually prefer to finance the direct costs of work with beneficiaries.

In principle, nonprofits can solve this problem by using unrestricted funds to cover indirect costs, but this is not a satisfying answer. Flexible funds should be conserved for other needs, such as seeding new initiatives or covering shortfalls in targeted fundraising. For instance, when an unexpected challenge or opportunity arises, unrestricted funds can serve as "bridge" financing, enabling the nonprofit to start addressing the new issue even before raising targeted donations for it. Yet a nonprofit cannot respond as nimbly if it uses all its flexible funds to pay for audits and fundraising.

So how should a nonprofit cover these indirect costs? The answer is to allocate them to specific programs, so targeted donations to these programs can cover them. For example, targeted donations to a college football team should fund not just direct costs (such as salaries for coaches, financial aid for athletes, and travel costs) but also indirect costs (such as maintenance costs for gyms and playing fields, fundraising expenses, and marketing costs). In other words, donors who love the football team should cover *all* of its costs.

The "quick and dirty" way to charge for overhead is a fixed percentage. With a 10 percent charge, for example, 90 percent of each targeted donation is allocated to direct costs and 10 percent to indirect costs. Yet the downside of a rough estimate is that costs are not separately stated and explained. As a result, donors are more likely to view them as a tax, instead of a necessary element of the work they value.

The better approach is to invest the time to identify and estimate each indirect cost—or, at least, as many of them as possible. Some programs have higher indirect costs than others, and a uniform percentage obscures these differences. For example, operating in conflict zones requires extra security, while working in countries where fraud is rampant requires extra internal controls, and the like.

By sharing detailed information about these various costs, a nonprofit treats donors as partners. Since they play a key role in the work, donors deserve to know what it involves. This transparency also can help the nonprofit make its case. When there clearly is a good reason for an expense, donors are more willing to pay it. Obviously, when there isn't a persuasive justification, nonprofits should find a way to avoid it.

This brings us to another advantage of a rigorous allocation of indirect costs: more informed decision-making. By digging into the details of indirect costs, a nonprofit sometimes finds ways to reduce them. More generally, to figure out how to spend scarce dollars, a nonprofit needs to know what each option *really* costs—not just the direct costs but the indirect ones as well. This more comprehensive accounting enables a nonprofit to make better decisions.

At the end of the day, these decisions should be dictated by the mission, not donor preferences. But donors can still pick what they want to fund, as long as they choose from a menu of initiatives the nonprofit already plans to run. With this approach, targeted donations can cover most of a nonprofit's budget, and unrestricted funds can be used sparingly to plug any gaps.

To sum up, the sixth "P" in this book, "partner," urges a nonprofit to treat donors like partners instead of cash machines. Funders need to see a nonprofit's problems as *their* problems and its successes as *their* successes. A nonprofit can nurture this personal commitment by showing donors the work firsthand, inviting them to help the nonprofit improve, involving them in the work, including them in a community of like-minded people, and offering choices about what they support. For each donor, some of these strategies are more compelling than others. Although the mix for each funder should be different, the goal should always be the same: donors need to feel like partners in the work.

Remember:

- A nonprofit can raise more money by treating donors as partners, so they see its problems as *their* problems. To nurture this feeling, nonprofits should engage donors in five different ways.
- **Inspiration**: First, a nonprofit should show donors the work, so they can see firsthand how their support change lives and advance ideals.
- **Improvements**: Second, a nonprofit also should tell donors how they can enhance this work, highlighting key challenges that funders can help to address.
- **Involvement**: Third, a nonprofit should offer funders opportunities to commit time as well as resources, inviting them to work with beneficiaries, brainstorm about problems, or make the case to other donors.
- **Integration**: Fourth, a nonprofit also should nurture a sense of community, encouraging donors to share experiences and forge ties with professionals, volunteers, beneficiaries, and each other.
- **Interests**: Finally, a nonprofit should offer donors a menu of options for their gift so they find something especially meaningful and feel connected to it.

CHAPTER 10

CONCLUSION

Saving the World Together

BRINGING OUT THE BEST in nonprofits isn't easy, but for many of us, it is a labor of love. We feel strongly about causes that matter to us. By advancing them, we stay true to our ideals, honor people we love, and bring hope and light into our lives.

I feel this way about the two nonprofits where I have worked, Columbia and JDC. My commitment to them is grounded not only in my enthusiasm for education and humanitarian work but also in my family's history. I was named after my paternal grandfather, so he looms especially large for me.

The other David Schizer was born at the turn of the twentieth century in Dzhuryn, a small village in Western Ukraine. His parents died when he was a young child. A few years later, his grandfather, who had been raising him and his two younger siblings, was murdered in a pogrom.

As a teenager, my grandfather became the "adult" responsible for his brother and sister. He eked out a meager living selling vegetables. According to family lore, this was not a good fit for him. His nose was constantly buried in a book, so he rarely noticed when goats would wander over and eat his inventory.

Meanwhile, the Russian revolution ignited a civil war between the Communists and monarchists. One day, some monarchists came to Dzhuryn. Not finding any Communists, they decided to murder some Jews. They lined up my grandfather and a few others against a wall. But before this makeshift firing squad could do its bloody work, a group of Communists suddenly appeared. As the "reds" and "whites" fired at each other, my grandfather and the others slipped away. This gut-wrenching experience persuaded him and his siblings to leave Ukraine for America.

During his first year in the United States, my grandfather lived on packages of peanuts while teaching himself English in the Brooklyn Public Library. After a brief stint as a peddler in Tennessee—not the right job for him, as his track record at the vegetable stand suggested—he returned to Brooklyn, met my grandmother, and enrolled at Columbia Teachers College. He earned a BA in 1928, the year my father was born, and an MA in 1930.

My grandfather was grateful to live in America, free of the persecution and violence he had known in Ukraine. To express his appreciation, he started a lifelong practice of paying more tax than he owed. As a tax lawyer, I can't say that I endorse this idea, but his patriotism resonates powerfully with me.

Unfortunately, years of sacrifice took a toll on my grandfather's health. He lost his eyesight as a young man. Because he had memorized the Bible as a child, he could make a living teaching in a Hebrew high school. One of his students, Norman Podhoretz, a prominent intellectual, remembered my grandfather fondly and told me what a wonderful teacher he was. Tragically, my grandfather had a massive heart attack in his mid-fifties and died a few years later.

I was born ten years after he died. Although my grandfather and I have the same name, our lives are astonishingly different. My childhood was also full of disappointment and loss, but my pain stemmed mainly from my devotion to the New York Mets. All joking aside, my comfortable life would be almost unrecognizable to my grandfather, but his choices made all the difference to me. By coming to America, he and the other immigrants in my family gave me opportunities they never had.

Obviously, I have no way to thank these relatives, who passed away years ago. So how can I repay this debt? The answer is to help other people who grapple with similar challenges and have the same dreams. The best way to do this is at nonprofits.

To honor my grandfather's memory, my father never forgot the Brooklyn Public Library's significance to his father—and, indeed, to countless others every day. For many years, my father took time away from his law practice to serve on the library's board of trustees, including as its chair.

For the same reason, I have always found special meaning in working at Columbia, knowing what the university has done for my family and for so many others. My grandfather is not my only relative whose life was transformed in Morningside Heights. My mother graduated from Barnard College and Columbia Law School. So for me, Columbia's mission of educating the next generation—and giving people opportunities they otherwise would never have had—is all the more fulfilling.

I have the same feeling about JDC. In 1914, the organization started helping people just like my grandfather. (As far as I know, he was never a JDC client.) Sadly, my grandfather's experience is not unique. Across the globe, hundreds of millions of people routinely face deprivation and violence. They need help, so JDC and other humanitarian organizations answer the call. Knowing what my own family once faced, I've been grateful for the chance to pitch in.

The key, of course, is to pitch in in the right way. Good intentions aren't enough. The point is not just to *feel* good but to *do* good. I realize that I sound like a "cranky uncle" again, but so be it. To add value, nonprofits need to be effective in advancing their missions.

It's heartbreaking when they waste money and miss opportunities. While this is also disappointing at for-profit firms, the stakes are different. When businesses underperform, they lose customers, the owners take a financial hit, and some employees lose their jobs. But when nonprofits let us down, their failings can echo throughout society. Urgent problems go unsolved, and chances to improve countless lives are missed.

Sadly, these sobering results are all too common. Some nonprofits pursue the wrong mission. Others have the right target in their sights, but their aim is off. Since the progress of nonprofits is hard to measure, their professionals and boards have more leeway to make bad choices. Some stick with outdated practices, put their own interests first, let expenses mount, and engage in pointless infighting. Instead of "the best of times," we have "the worst of times" at these nonprofits.

Fortunately, it doesn't have to be this way. To bring out the best in nonprofits, we need to accomplish two things. First, we have to figure out the best way to advance their mission. Second, we need buy-in for this strategy.

This book has offered guidance on these twin goals. To achieve them, nonprofits should rely on the "Six Ps" I've outlined in these pages:

- **Plan**: With the right planning process, nonprofits rethink their work and get buy-in for their new plan.
- **Persevere**: To get others on board, we need to set the right pace, line up allies, and win over (or at least placate) skeptics. We have to pick our battles. But on major issues, we need to be true to our principles.
- **Prioritize**: Instead of just following the money, nonprofits should figure out how they can add the most value. With "the three questions," they target urgent needs, respond in impactful and cost-effective ways, and focus on their comparative advantages. This way, they prioritize socially valuable work that others can't or won't do as well.

- **Pivot:** Nonprofits should experiment with different ways to advance their mission. Along with hiring and retaining the right people, they need to rethink what they do and how they do it.
- **Publicize:** Every year, nonprofits should share a new plan with the public. This transparency disseminates good ideas, motivates nonprofits to deliver results, and empowers donors and others to be more effective monitors.
- **Partner:** To raise more money, nonprofits should treat donors as partners, involving them in the work, ushering them into a community, and letting them choose what they support.

The truth is, the "Six Ps" aren't for the faint of heart. I am reminded of what one of my favorite law school professors Geoffrey Hazard used to tell us about the challenges of practicing law. "Well, my dears," he would say, "I never promised you a rose garden."

The same is true at nonprofits. It's easy to love their mission, but much harder to advance it effectively. There are no shortcuts. Inevitably, there will be knotty problems and disappointments along the way. But in my experience, there is still ample reason for hope. With rigorous analysis, tireless advocacy, and a bit of luck, we can deliver inspiring results. By following the six (not so easy) steps in this book, we can save the world together.

ACKNOWLEDGMENTS

MY THANKS TO THE distinguished nonprofit leaders who agreed to be interviewed for this book. Their insights enriched it in so many ways, and their commitment and professionalism shined through in all of our conversations.

I also owe a great debt to countless professionals, board members, and donors at Columbia University and the American Jewish Joint Distribution Committee (JDC), who have taught me so much over the years and whose talent and dedication were indispensable to our many successes together. I've also learned many valuable lessons from wise colleagues who have served with me on a number of for-profit and nonprofit boards—too many to mention here.

I also appreciate valuable comments on the manuscript and insightful guidance I've received from Robert Abrams, Aviad Bodner, Alexandra Carter, Zach Fasman, Jeff Gordon, Zohar Goshen, David Greenwald, Philip Hamburger, Michael Heller, Kate Judge, Louis Kaplow, Gillian Lester, Reynold Levy, Oivind Lorentzen, Henry Monaghan, Asher Ostrin, Stan Rabin, Alex Raskolnikov, Dena Rashes, Dean Reuter, Henry Timms, Meredith Wolf Schizer, Nina Shenker, and Tim Wu. My thanks also to Megan Sullivan for her capable research assistance, as well as to students in my class on nonprofits at Columbia Law School, whose thoughtful reactions to draft chapters were invaluable.

I am grateful to the Richard Paul Richman Center for Business, Law, and Public Policy at Columbia University and to the Columbia

Law School Center for Israeli Legal Studies for generously supporting this book.

My thanks also to my agent, Karen Gantz, as well as to Adam Bellow, Olivia Brothers, Aleigha Kely, Barbara Pepe, Emma Venker, and the team at Post Hill Press.

Last but not least, I owe a profound debt to my family. My parents, Hazel and Zevie Schizer, helped to inspire my commitment to nonprofits. Meredith and our children have reinforced that commitment, and also have (almost) always been understanding when I've had to work late, travel, answer endless emails, spend hours on the phone, and otherwise try to "save the world."

The ideas in this book are my personal views. They do not represent the views of Columbia University, JDC, or any other institution with which I have been affiliated. Any errors are my own.

David M. Schizer
New York City

ABOUT THE AUTHOR

DAVID M. SCHIZER IS a twenty-five year veteran of the nonprofit world and became the youngest dean in Columbia Law School's history at age thirty-five. He was also the CEO of JDC, a humanitarian organization active in seventy countries with a $365 million annual budget. Schizer has served on the board of a number of nonprofits and for-profit companies, including 92NY, the Ramaz School, the *Philadelphia Inquirer*, Feil Properties, and SEACOR Holdings.

A member of the Columbia Law School faculty since 1998, Schizer is a leading scholar of nonprofits, tax, energy, and business law, as well as an award-winning teacher. He has taught at Yale, Harvard, Hebrew University, University of Tokyo, and other major universities around the world. Schizer also clerked for US Supreme Court Justice Ruth Bader Ginsburg and Court of Appeals Judge Alex Kozinski.

Schizer has a BA, MA, and JD from Yale. He lives in New York City with his wife and three children.

Made in the USA
Middletown, DE
18 February 2024

49305842R00139